Systems Understanding Aid

8TH EDITION

REFERENCE

Alvin A. Arens, Ph.D., C.P.A.
PricewaterhouseCoopers Auditing Professor, Emeritus (dec)
Michigan State University

D. Dewey Ward, Ph.D.
Professor of Accounting, Emeritus
Michigan State University

2012

PREFACE

OBJECTIVES

The overall objective of the *Systems Understanding Aid* is to help students understand and visualize the entire accounting process for a simple company using a manual accounting system. Accounting students frequently have difficulty understanding how various parts of the accounting process tie together for the preparation of financial statements. Once students are able to visualize the entire process, it is easier for them to understand more complex accounting concepts and methods, and how they affect financial statements. It is also essential for students interested in auditing to understand the accounting process.

Another objective is to help students learn about commonly used business documents. It is common for accounting students to graduate from a college or university and not understand the purposes or uses of documents such as receiving reports and vendors' invoices. The *Systems Understanding Aid* is intended to overcome this shortcoming of accounting education.

A final objective is to help students learn about flowcharting and key internal controls as a part of understanding documents, records, and accounting systems. Flowcharting, documents, records, and internal controls are so closely related that it is beneficial for students to study them at the same time.

The *Systems Understanding Aid* is intended as a supplement for a financial accounting, auditing, or systems course. Students who do not have a good understanding of business documents and records or how accounting transactions are documented, recorded, and summarized will receive significant benefit.

CONTENT

The materials are made up of two parts: Reference and Project.

Reference. The Reference describes the role and nature of documents and records and key internal controls in a typical small company using a manual accounting system. There are two options for using the Reference. The Reference can be studied in detail before beginning the Project. The advantage of this approach is that it increases the level of understanding of the accounting process before beginning the Project. Alternatively, the user can begin the Project immediately and refer to the Reference only when there is a question about a document, record, or systems procedure. The advantage of this approach is that it takes less time to complete the Project. However, this approach should be adopted only if the user has a reasonably good understanding of the accounting process and related documents and records.

Several distinct features of the Reference are:

- The Reference ties directly to the Project.
- Simplicity is emphasized throughout.
- The relationships among financial statements, journals, documents, and records are clearly illustrated.
- Flowcharting and internal controls are explained and illustrated.
- Each major transaction segment in a typical company is discussed and interrelated with other segments.
- The preparation of trial balances (such as general ledger, accounts receivable, and fixed assets), bank reconciliations, and financial statements is discussed and illustrated.

Project. The Project requires recording transactions and preparing documents, records, and financial statements based on information provided in the instructions. The use of the Project is based on two learning concepts: (1) students learn better by doing than by reading or listening, and (2) excess repetition results in boredom and wasted time rather than learning.

The Project has the following important characteristics:

- Actual documents, obtained from a business forms company, are used throughout, not copies or facsimiles.
- Multi-copy and multi-color documents are used wherever they are commonly found in business.

- Journals, subsidiary ledgers, and general ledgers are included.

- Flowcharts include instructions that must be followed to complete the Project properly.

- The small number of transactions minimizes repetition.

- Major documents, journals, and ledgers that are most likely to be encountered by accountants are included.

- Tie-in is made among documents, journals, ledgers, and worksheet reconciliations.

- The materials included in your *Systems Understanding Aid* package are the only materials needed to complete all requirements.

The Project contains three parts. The first part is a separate booklet of instructions, flowcharts, and ledgers. The instructions should be read carefully before starting the Project. The second part includes journals, documents, and related records that must be prepared by following the instructions and using the flowcharts. The third part is a set of file tabs kept in the envelope that is used for filing documents according to the instructions. All of the materials are to be turned in to the instructor in the envelope in which the *Systems Understanding Aid* is packaged.

AUTHORS' EXPERIENCE

The original *Systems Understanding Aid* included a few simple transactions and copies of documents. The response from students was so positive that we gradually expanded it to include more realistic documents, flowcharting, and a few simple internal controls. The response from students to the revision was even more positive.

The underlying concept has continued to emphasize the role of documents and records, their relationship to financial statements, and the relationship of general ledger control accounts to supporting working papers. We have found that students understand concepts far better after they understand typical systems, documents, and records.

MANUAL VERSUS COMPUTERIZED SYSTEMS

Most accounting systems used in business and other organizations today are computerized. It is therefore legitimate to inquire about the benefits of studying manual systems. There are three primary benefits.

First, the objectives and information recorded in manual and computerized systems are essentially the same. It is easier to understand manual systems because it is possible to see what happens in the documentation and recording process. This knowledge helps students understand computerized systems.

Second, the documents used for many computerized systems are similar to those used in manual systems. For example, both computerized and manual systems use documents such as receiving reports, checks, and shipping documents. These documents are explained in the *Systems Understanding Aid*.

Third, the flow of documents and records and the related internal controls are often the same in manual and computerized systems. For example, the approval of purchase orders by an authorized person is common for any type of accounting system. The flowlines used in the *Systems Understanding Aid* and the performance requirements are intended to help students understand the flow of documents and records and the related internal controls. Even the Big 4 accounting firms include manual accounting activities in their training programs to help auditors understand the flow of information and related controls.

ACKNOWLEDGMENTS

The extensive involvement of Carol Borsum in all aspects of the project is greatly appreciated. Also appreciated is the help of Lynne Wood for word processing in preparation of the manuscript and of Patricia Naretta for proofreading and other assistance.

Finally, the encouragement and continuing support of family, friends, and associates have contributed in large measure to the completion of this book.

TABLE OF CONTENTS

TABLE OF FIGURES

CHAPTER 1

Overview of the Accounting System

This book is about the documents, records, and processes used by companies to originate, approve, and record transactions. Chapter 1 shows the relationship between the main steps of the accounting process, from the origin of transactions to the preparation of financial statements. Subsequent chapters show how each of these steps is applied to different types of transactions, such as sales and cash receipts.

FINANCIAL STATEMENTS

Figure 1-1 (pages 8 and 9) includes the financial statements of Simple Example Company for the years ended December 31, 2013 and 2014. For simplicity, the footnotes have not been included. The remainder of the text material will demonstrate how the information for Simple's financial statements is derived. A small company is used to make it practical to show the documents, records, and source of all information for the statements.

The auditor's report indicates that an audit was done by a CPA firm and that the statements were determined to be fairly stated, in accordance with generally accepted accounting principles (GAAP). A CPA firm cannot indicate that the statements are fairly stated unless footnotes are included. For these purposes, assume that the footnotes are there.

NATURE OF TRANSACTIONS

Financial statements represent the accumulated total of all accounting transactions in which the company has been involved since its inception. A company records transactions and periodically summarizes them in accordance with generally accepted accounting principles. Transactions affecting the balance sheet are carried forward from year to year, whereas those affecting the income statement are closed to stockholders' equity annually.

Transactions are the exchanges between a company and another party, or adjustments to recorded accounting information, that must be reflected in the financial statements in accordance with accounting principles. Examples of transactions are: a sale to a customer, a purchase of equipment, and a write-off of an uncollectible account receivable. Recording transactions requires five essential steps:

1. Identify the exchanges or adjustments that must be recorded.

2. Determine which account balances are affected by the exchanges or adjustments.

3. Assign proper values to the transactions for each account.

4. Record the transactions in the proper time period.

5. Record the transactions in the accounting records, and summarize them into the financial statements.

You have already studied accounting transactions in principles and intermediate accounting. It is assumed throughout this text that you already understand the first four steps in recording transactions. The emphasis in the Project and Reference is on the documentation, recording, and summarizing of the transactions.

FIGURE 1-1
Comparative Financial Statements and Audit Report of Simple Example Company

SIMPLE EXAMPLE COMPANY
BALANCE SHEET
AT DECEMBER 31, 2013 AND 2012

ASSETS

	2013	2012
CURRENT ASSETS		
Cash	$ 83	$ 93
Accounts receivable - less allowance for doubtful accounts of $41 in 2013 and $41 in 2012	231	226
Inventory	114	126
Prepaid rent	4	7
Total current assets	432	452
FIXED ASSETS - Less accumulated depreciation of $60 in 2013 and $45 in 2012	0	15
Total assets	$ 432	$ 467

LIABILITIES AND STOCKHOLDERS' EQUITY

	2013	2012
CURRENT LIABILITIES		
Accounts payable	$ 158	$ 135
Note payable - current portion	0	12
Wages and salaries payable	12	0
Payroll taxes withheld and payable	20	17
Total Liabilities	190	164
STOCKHOLDERS' EQUITY		
Common stock (50 shares issued and outstanding)	200	200
Retained earnings	42	103
Total stockholders' equity	242	303
Total liabilities and stockholders' equity	$ 432	$ 467

SIMPLE EXAMPLE COMPANY
STATEMENT OF INCOME AND RETAINED EARNINGS
YEARS ENDED DECEMBER 31, 2013 AND 2012

	2013	2012
REVENUE		
Sales	$3,648	$3,614
Less: Sales returns and allowances	214	326
Sales discounts taken	182	147
Net sales	3,252	3,141
COST OF GOODS SOLD		
Beginning inventory	126	118
Purchases	2,120	2,044
Goods available for sale	2,246	2,162
Less: Ending inventory	114	126
Cost of goods sold	2,132	2,036
GROSS MARGIN	1,120	1,105
OPERATING EXPENSES		
Wages and salaries	729	693
Payroll taxes	101	90
Rent, repairs, & utilities	179	144
Postage and travel	106	113
Bad debt expense	49	37
Depreciation	15	12
Total operating expenses	1,179	1,089
OPERATING INCOME (LOSS)	(59)	16
NONOPERATING EXPENSE-INTEREST	2	3
INCOME (LOSS) BEFORE TAXES	(61)	13
FEDERAL INCOME TAXES	0	3
NET INCOME (LOSS)	(61)	10
RETAINED EARNINGS - Beginning of year	103	99
DIVIDENDS	0	6
RETAINED EARNINGS - End of year	$ 42	$ 103
EARNINGS PER COMMON SHARE	$(1.22)	$ .20

FIGURE 1-1 (cont.)

SIMPLE EXAMPLE COMPANY
INDEPENDENT AUDITOR'S REPORT

To the Board of Directors
Simple Example Company

We have audited the accompanying balance sheets of Simple Example Company as of December 31, 2013 and 2012, and the related statements of income and retained earnings and cash flows for the years then ended. These financial statements are the responsibility of the Company's management. Our responsibility is to express an opinion on these financial statements based on our audits.

We conducted our audits in accordance with auditing standards generally accepted in the United States of America. Those standards require that we plan and perform the audit to obtain reasonable assurance about whether the financial statements are free of material misstatement. An audit includes examining, on a test basis, evidence supporting the amounts and disclosures in the financial statements. An audit also includes assessing the accounting principles used and significant estimates made by management, as well as evaluating the overall financial statement presentation. We believe that our audits provide a reasonable basis for our opinion.

In our opinion, the financial statements referred to above present fairly, in all material respects, the financial position of Simple Example Company as of December 31, 2013 and 2012, and the results of its operations and its cash flows for the years then ended in conformity with accounting principles generally accepted in the United States of America.

Ketchem, Cheatin & Hurtum

CERTIFIED PUBLIC ACCOUNTANTS
February 19, 2014

SIMPLE EXAMPLE COMPANY
STATEMENT OF CASH FLOWS
AT DECEMBER 31, 2013 AND 2012

	2013	2012
CASH FLOWS FROM OPERATING ACTIVITIES		
Net income (loss)	$ (61)	$ 10
Adjustments to reconcile net income (loss) to net cash from operating activities:		
Depreciation	15	12
(Increase) decrease in assets:		
Accounts receivable	(5)	5
Inventory	12	8
Prepaid rent	3	(4)
Increase (decrease) in liabilities:		
Accounts payable	23	(7)
Wages and salaries payable	12	(3)
Payroll taxes withheld and payable	3	2
Net cash provided by operating activities	2	23
CASH FLOWS FROM INVESTING ACTIVITIES		
Cash payments for fixed assets	0	(7)
CASH FLOWS FROM FINANCING ACTIVITIES		
Payments on notes payable	(12)	(7)
Dividends	0	(6)
Net cash used in financing activities	(12)	(13)
NET INCREASE (DECREASE) IN CASH	$ (10)	$ 3
CASH - Beginning of year	93	90
CASH - End of year	$ 83	$ 93
NONCASH INVESTING ACTIVITIES		
Purchases of fixed assets with note payable	—	$ 5

STEPS IN THE ACCOUNTING PROCESS

There are several steps after the occurrence of transactions until their inclusion in financial statements. Accountants are typically involved in each step. Frequently management and other employees are responsible for the transactions or participate in the process in some manner.

The flow diagram below summarizes the nine steps.

When accounting students lack an understanding of each of these steps and the relationship between the steps, it is a hindrance to understanding accounting and auditing. Each component of the flow diagram is addressed individually in the subsections of the narrative that follows.

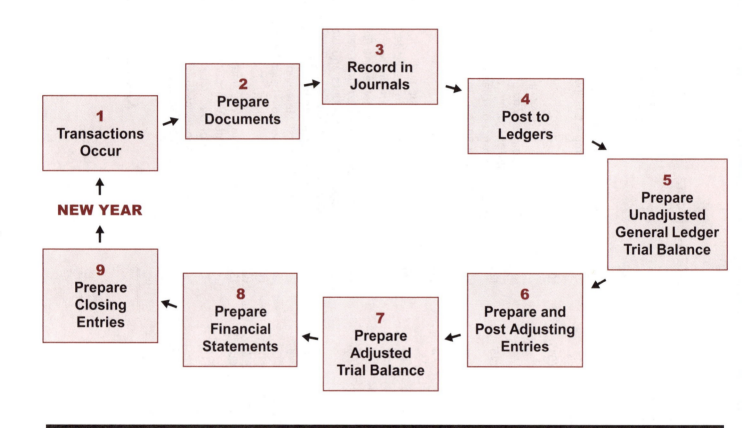

Figure 1-2 identifies the three most common transaction cycles or transaction systems. The effects on financial statements resulting from transactions in each cycle for Simple Example Company are also shown. The transaction cycles identified are an oversimplification of actual business practice.

Types of transactions vary from one business to another. A retail meat market, a manufacturer of automobiles, a CPA firm, and an insurance company each have different types of transactions. For Simple Example Company, however, the three transaction cycles are sufficient.

FIGURE 1-2
Transaction Cycles and Their Effect on Financial Statement Balances

Three Most Common Transaction Cycles	Financial Statement Balances of Simple Example Company Affected by the Class of Transactions	
	Balance Sheet	Income Statement
Sales and cash receipts	Cash Accounts receivable Allowance for doubtful accounts Common stock	Sales Sales returns and allowances Bad debt expense Sales discounts taken
Purchases and cash disbursements (purchase of goods and services and cash disbursements, excluding payroll)	Cash Inventory Prepaid rent Fixed assets Accumulated depreciation Accounts payable Interest payable	Purchases Rent Repair Postage Travel Utilities Freight-in
Payroll (purchase of employee services and disbursements for those services)	Cash Wages and salaries payable Federal income taxes withheld FICA taxes payable Other payroll taxes payable	Wages and salaries expense Payroll tax expense

2
Prepare Documents

The preparation and use of documents are essential to the effective conduct of business and accounting for that business activity. Many types of documents are used in business and they serve several purposes. Examples of documents and their purposes are shown below. Many others are used in the Project.

DOCUMENT	PURPOSE
Payroll time card that includes hours worked and authorization for payment.	Used to determine gross pay owed to employee.
Customer purchase order including quantity ordered and agreed-upon price.	Used to determine quantities to ship to customer and amount to bill.
Sales invoice that includes the total amount of sale.	Provides information to customer and for recording sales transaction.
Monthly bank statement.	Provides information to determine whether the company or bank has errors or omissions in recording cash receipts and disbursements.

A useful distinction between different documents is their source: internally or externally prepared. An internally prepared document is prepared by the company for which you are preparing the financial statements. Examples are a purchase order to buy inventory and a payroll time card to accumulate hours for payment of payroll. An externally prepared document is prepared by an outside organization doing business with your company. Examples are an order to buy goods from your company (customer purchase order) or a sales invoice requesting payment for repair services provided to your company (vendor's invoice).

A second distinction about documents is when they are prepared, relative to when the transaction occurs. Documents can be prepared before a transaction occurs, at the same time it occurs, or after the transaction is completed. Examples of each situation and the nature of the action creating the need for a document are shown in Figure 1-3.

FIGURE 1-3
Typical Timing of Document Preparation for Different Types of Actions

Typical Time of Document Preparation	Nature of Action Causing Need for a Document	Example
Document prepared before transaction occurs	1. Issue order to buy goods or services 2. Receive order for a sale of goods or services	1. Purchase order 2. Customer purchase order
Document prepared at same time transaction occurs	1. Receive goods or services 2. Deliver goods	1. Receiving report 2. Bill of lading/Shipping document
Document prepared after transaction occurs	1. Send bill for goods or services sold 2. Receive bill for goods or services purchased	1. Sales invoice 2. Vendor's invoice

3
Record in Journals

Journals are used for the initial recording of individual transactions. Individual transactions can be recorded directly in the journals, or they can be totaled and only the totals included in the journals. There are four essential characteristics of journals:

1. Every transaction occurring during an accounting period should be recorded in a journal. Transactions should not be transferred from documents directly to the general ledger. The use of journals to record all transactions minimizes the likelihood of failing to record transactions and makes it easier to subsequently determine what was recorded.

2. Journals follow the requirements of a double-entry recording system. Debits and credits for each transaction must be

equal. For example, if fixed assets are acquired for $226 cash, the transaction must be recorded as a debit to fixed assets of $226 and a credit to cash of an equal amount.

3. Most companies use a general journal and several special journals. The special journals are a convenient way to summarize similar, repetitive types of transactions such as sales, cash receipts, and purchases. These journals provide chronological listings and monthly summaries of the related transactions. They are important sources of transactions history and make it faster and easier to find and review such transactions at a later date. They also provide quick reference information for management. The general journal is used for mostly non-repetitive transactions such as error corrections, adjusting entries, and transactions not appropriate for any of the special journals.

4. The number and titles of journals for different companies vary with the accounting information needs and system design preferences of management. Figure 1-4 illustrates the typical journal titles and the nature of transactions usually recorded in each journal.

FIGURE 1-4
Typical Journals and Nature of Transactions Included

Typical Title	Other Common Titles	Nature of Transactions Typically Recorded
Sales journal (SJ)	Revenue journal Cash sales journal Accounts receivable journal	Sales or other revenue* Sales returns and allowances may be recorded here or in a separate journal
Cash receipts journal (CR)	Receipts register Cash journal	All cash receipts*
Purchases journal (PJ)	Acquisitions journal Purchase register Voucher register Accounts payable journal	All purchases of goods and services except payroll* Purchase returns and allowances may be recorded here or in a separate journal
Cash disbursements journal (CD)	Disbursement journal Check register Cash journal Payments record	All cash disbursements made by check except payroll*
Payroll journal (PR)	Payroll register	All payroll disbursements (usually made by check)
General journal (GJ)	Miscellaneous journal	Error corrections, adjusting entries, closing entries, and other transactions not recorded in other journals

*At the discretion of the person designing the accounting system, sales made for cash can be recorded in either the cash receipts journal or the sales journal, and purchases made for cash can be recorded in either the cash disbursements journal or the purchases journal.

General Ledger. The general ledger summarizes the transactions in journals by account balances. Some of the characteristics of the general ledger are as follows:

- The number and description of general ledger accounts depend on the needs of management. Some companies have hundreds of accounts; others have only a few. The account titles for a company are included in the **chart of accounts**. The chart of accounts for Simple Example Company is shown in Figure 1-5.

- All transactions must be transferred (posted) from the journals to the general ledger periodically, usually monthly. For specialized journals, such as the sales journal, the transactions are totaled monthly in each journal for each account. Only the total is posted to the general ledger. For the general journal, individual transactions are posted to the general ledger. The reason is that general journal transactions vary considerably, which results in few common ledger accounts and no totals to post.

FIGURE 1-5
Chart of Accounts
Simple Example Company

Current Assets
101	Cash in bank
102	Payroll cash
103	Accounts receivable
104	Allowance for doubtful accounts
105	Inventory
106	Prepaid rent

Fixed Assets
201	Delivery equipment
202	Accumulated depreciation

Current Liabilities
301	Accounts payable
302	Wages and salaries payable
303	Payroll taxes payable
304	Rent payable
305	Withholding taxes payable
306	FICA taxes payable
307	Dividends payable

Long-term Liabilities
401	Notes payable

Stockholders' Equity
501	Common stock
502	Paid-in capital in excess of par
503	Retained earnings
504	Dividends

Revenues
601	Sales
602	Miscellaneous revenue
603	Sales returns and allowances
604	Sales discounts taken

Expenses
701	Cost of goods sold
702	Purchases
703	Purchases discounts
704	Purchases returns and allowances
705	Rent expense
706	Repair expense
707	Utility expense
708	Postage expense
709	Depreciation expense
710	Travel expense
711	Bad debt expense
712	Wages and salaries expense–administrative
713	Wages and salaries expense–selling
714	Employer's FICA expense
715	Other payroll tax expense
716	Miscellaneous expense
717	Income tax expense
718	Interest expense

800   Income Summary

- The general ledger includes the accumulated net total of all transactions, by account balance, since the inception of the company. For example, the cash-in-bank balance is the net of cash receipts and cash disbursements since the company started. Revenue and expense transactions are closed to a stockholders' equity account at the end of the year. For a corporation, the stockholders' equity account is retained earnings.

Subsidiary Ledgers. Some general ledger accounts have too much activity and detail to be efficiently used as one general ledger account. Detail is usually kept in a subsidiary ledger, which acts as support to the general ledger and agrees in total to the corresponding general ledger account.

A company could choose to have no subsidiary ledger accounts, but the likely effect would be to have a large number of accounts in the general ledger or insufficient detailed information to manage the company properly.

To illustrate, one common type of subsidiary ledger is for accounts receivable. If a company had only two accounts receivable, it could have two general ledger accounts called accounts receivable A and accounts receivable B.

It is impractical to have a general ledger account for each customer if there are hundreds of accounts receivable. Nevertheless, a record must be kept of the amount due from each customer. The record keeping is done by using subsidiary accounts. Each account in the accounts receivable subsidiary ledger represents a customer. The total of the subsidiary ledger account balances agrees to the general ledger accounts receivable balance. Common subsidiary records and their related subsidiary ledgers and general ledger control accounts are shown in Figure 1-6.

FIGURE 1-6
Common Subsidiary Records,
Related Subsidiary Ledgers, and Related General Ledger Control Accounts

Examples of Subsidiary Records	Subsidiary Ledger / Control Account in GL
Accounts receivable from each customer	AR subsidiary ledger / Accounts receivable
Accounts payable to each vendor	AP subsidiary ledger / Accounts payable
Cost of individual delivery equipment assets	Fixed asset subsidiary ledger / Delivery equipment
Depreciation expense on individual delivery equipment assets	Fixed asset subsidiary ledger / Depreciation expense
Accumulated depreciation on individual delivery equipment assets	Fixed asset subsidiary ledger / Accumulated depreciation – delivery equipment
Record of employee wages and deductions/ withholdings	Employee earnings subsidiary ledger / Wages & salaries expense
Perpetual record for each type of inventory	Perpetual inventory subsidiary ledger / Inventory

In posting from journals to ledgers for accounts with subsidiary ledgers, it is necessary to post the same amounts to both the general ledger and related subsidiary ledgers. Otherwise the total of the subsidiary ledger accounts won't equal the balance in the general ledger. This is accomplished by posting only the totals from journals to the general ledger. Individual transactions are posted to the related subsidiary ledger accounts. In that way, the detail is shown in the subsidiary ledgers and the total is shown in the general ledger control account. Figure 1-7 (page 16) illustrates the way this is done for the accounts receivable account.

Observe in Figure 1-7 that:

- The debit to accounts receivable for each sales transaction is posted to a subsidiary account, whereas the total is posted to the accounts receivable general ledger account.

- The accounts receivable aged trial balance is prepared from the balances in the subsidiary ledger accounts.

- The total of the accounts receivable aged trial balance must equal the accounts receivable general ledger balance.

Accounts receivable collections recorded in the cash receipts journal are posted to the accounts receivable general ledger and subsidiary ledger accounts in the same manner as described for sales transactions. The same is true of sales returns and allowances.

For transactions in the general journal that affect an account with a subsidiary ledger account, the transactions must be posted to both the general and subsidiary ledgers.

FIGURE 1-7
Relationships of Journals
to Subsidiary and General Ledgers

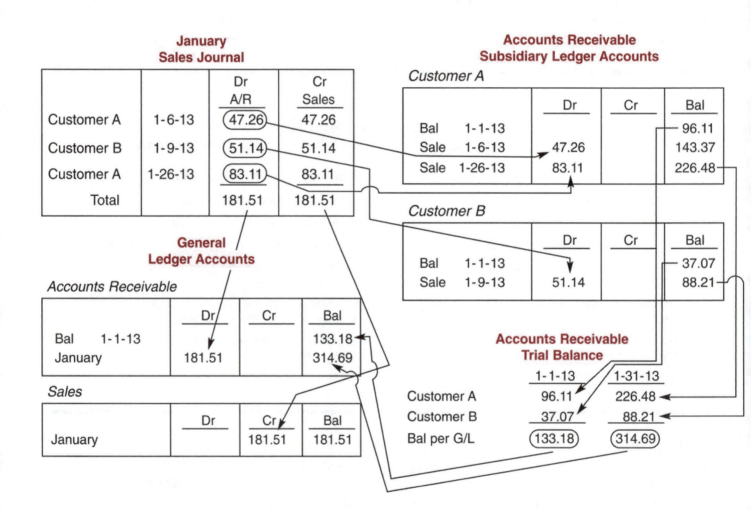

A general ledger trial balance is a listing of general ledger account balances at a point of time, with the debits in one column and the credits in another. The total debits must equal the total credits. If they don't, the error in the general ledger or trial balance should be corrected. A trial balance is typically prepared whenever a company plans to prepare financial statements. A distinction should be made between an unadjusted and an adjusted trial balance. An unadjusted trial balance is the listing of account balances in the general ledger before adjusting journal entries are made for month- and year-end accruals, prepayments, and errors. An adjusted trial balance is the listing of account balances after all adjustments are made.

An unadjusted trial balance is prepared only as an aid in preparing adjusting entries and financial statements. Most accountants can prepare financial statements more efficiently after information is summarized on one or two pages rather than in the more detailed general ledger.

The most common method used by accountants to list the unadjusted trial balance is a worksheet. A worksheet is illustrated for Simple Example Company in Figure 1-8 (page 18). Although Figure 1-8 is a year-end worksheet, a similar worksheet can be prepared monthly or quarterly. Notice that the worksheet typically includes the following columns:

- Account Number
- Account Title
- Prior Year Post-Closing Trial Balance — debit and credit columns
- Current Year Unadjusted Trial Balance — debit and credit columns
- Adjustments — debit and credit columns
- Adjusted Trial Balance — debit and credit columns
- Income Statement — debit and credit columns
- Balance Sheet — debit and credit columns

Columns 3 and 4 are the current year's unadjusted trial balance for Simple Example Company. Those account balances were taken directly from the general ledger. The unadjusted trial balance should not be prepared until all transactions, except adjusting entries, have been recorded in the journals and posted to the general and subsidiary ledgers. If the debits and credits in the unadjusted trial balance are not equal, it is inappropriate to continue until the error or errors are corrected. Similarly, the debits must equal the credits in the adjustments columns and the adjusted trial balance columns.

FIGURE 1-8
SIMPLE EXAMPLE COMPANY
Year-End Worksheet
December 31, 2013

ACC. NO.	ACCOUNT TITLE	12-31-12 POST-CLOSING TRIAL BALANCE Dr	Cr	12-31-13 UNADJUSTED TRIAL BALANCE Dr	Cr	ADJUSTMENTS Dr	Cr	ADJUSTED TRIAL BALANCE Dr	Cr	INCOME STATEMENT Dr	Cr	BALANCE SHEET Dr	Cr
101	Cash in bank	88		78				78				78	
102	Payroll cash	5		5				5				5	
103	Accounts receivable	267		298			(2) 26	272				272	
104	Allowance for doubtful accounts		41		18	(2) 26	(1) 49		41				41
105	Inventory	126		126			(8) 12	114				114	
106	Prepaid rent	7		8			(3) 4	4				4	
201	Delivery equipment	60		60				60				60	
202	Accumulated depreciation		45		45		(4) 15		60				60
301	Accounts payable		135		158				158				158
302	Wages and salaries payable		-0-		-0-		(5) 12		12				12
303	Payroll taxes payable		3		-0-		(6) 4		4				4
304	Rent payable		-0-		-0-				-0-				
305	Withholding taxes payable		5		6				6				6
306	FICA taxes payable		9		5		(7) 5		10				10
307	Dividends payable		-0-		-0-				-0-				
401	Notes payable		12		-0-				-0-				
501	Common stock		200		200				200				200
502	Paid-in capital in excess of par		-0-		-0-				-0-				
503	Retained earnings		103		103				103				103
504	Dividends	-0-		-0-				-0-					
601	Sales				3,648				3,648		3,648		
602	Miscellaneous revenue				-0-				-0-				
603	Sales returns and allowances			214				214		214			
604	Sales discounts taken			182				182		182			
701	Cost of goods sold			-0-		(8) 2,132		2,132		2,132			
702	Purchases			2,166			(8) 2,166	-0-					
703	Purchases discounts				46	(8) 46			-0-				
704	Purchases returns and allowances				-0-				-0-				
705	Rent expense			44		(3) 4		48		48			
706	Repair expense			69				69		69			
707	Utility expense			62				62		62			
708	Postage expense			49				49		49			
709	Depreciation expense			-0-		(4) 15		15		15			
710	Travel expense			57				57		57			
711	Bad debt expense			-0-		(1) 49		49		49			
712	Wages and salaries expense - admin.			264		(5) 6		270		270			
713	Wages and salaries expense - selling			453		(5) 6		459		459			
714	Employer's FICA expense			51		(7) 5		56		56			
715	Other payroll tax expense			41		(6) 4		45		45			
716	Miscellaneous expense			-0-				-0-					
717	Income tax expense			-0-				-0-					
718	Interest expense			2				2		2			
	Subtotals	553	553	4,330	4,330	2,303	2,303	4,242	4,242	3,709	3,648	533	594
800	Income Summary - Net Income (Loss)									(61)			(61)
	TOTALS	553	553	4,330	4,330	2,303	2,303	4,242	4,242	3,648	3,648	533	533

Handwritten annotations (Balance Sheet): 83, 231, 20

Handwritten annotations (Income Statement): 179, 106, 729, 101

The primary reason for preparing adjusting entries is to convert from the cash basis of accounting to the accrual basis. Most transactions are recorded in the journals on the accrual basis. An example is recording the purchase of inventory when the merchandise is received rather than when it is paid for. However, for many types of transactions it is more convenient to finalize the conversion to the accrual basis with adjusting entries. These are illustrated in this section.

The following are important requirements in recording adjusting entries:

- Adjusting entries are prepared only at the end of the period when a company plans to prepare financial statements. Some companies prepare statements monthly, others quarterly, and some only annually.

- Every adjusting entry affects both the balance sheet and the income statement.

- The total debits and credits must be equal for each adjusting entry.

- All adjusting entries are first recorded in the general journal. No other journal is used for adjusting entries.

- Each adjusting entry is prepared separately.

- Each amount in each adjusting entry is posted individually to the appropriate general ledger account.

- Most adjusting entries are not posted to subsidiary ledgers.

There are six general categories of adjusting entries:

- Prepaid expense — an expense paid for in advance of its use. An example is paying several months' rent in advance. The accrual accounting method requires that rent expense be recorded in the period in which the asset is used rather than the period in which the cash payment is made. Prepaid expense involves adjustment of both an asset and an expense account.

- Accrued expense — an expense incurred for which payment has not been made. An example is paying rent after it is due. It is the opposite of a prepaid expense. For prepaids, cash is paid before the expense is incurred; for accrued expenses, cash is paid after the expense is incurred. Accrued expenses involve adjusting a liability and an expense account.

- Accrued revenue — a revenue earned for which the cash has not yet been received. An example is interest revenue on a note receivable. An accrued revenue is similar to an accrued expense, except it involves revenue rather than expense. Accrued revenue involves adjusting an asset and a revenue account.

- Unearned revenue — a revenue received in cash in advance of being earned. An example is receiving an interest payment on a note before it is due. Unearned revenue is the opposite of accrued revenue. For unearned revenue, cash is received before the revenue is earned; for accrued revenue, cash is received after it is earned. Unearned revenue involves adjusting a liability and a revenue account.

- Estimated items — an expense recorded on the basis of estimates. Examples include bad debt expense, federal income tax expense, and depreciation expense. An adjusting entry for estimated items includes adjusting an expense account and an asset or a liability account.

• Inventory adjustment — under the periodic inventory method, the ending inventory must be recorded. At the same time the account balances in purchases, purchase returns and allowances, freight-in, and purchase discounts are transferred to cost of goods sold. The debit part of the adjusting entry includes ending inventory, cost of goods sold, purchase returns and allowances, and discounts. The credit part includes beginning inventory, purchases, and freight-in. The adjusting entry for inventory has some characteristics of a closing entry, however, it is more convenient to call the inventory adjustment an adjusting entry. (Closing is discussed in the next section. Inventories are discussed more fully in Chapter 6.)

Figure 1-9 summarizes the six categories of adjusting journal entries. Figure 1-10 shows the eight adjusting entries for Simple Example Company as they are recorded in the general journal.

Although the general journal includes all adjusting entries, it can also include other transactions. For example, it is common to record bank service charges in the general journal even though this is not an adjusting entry.

FIGURE 1-9
Categories of Adjusting Entries

Category	Balance Sheet Account	Income Statement Account	Type of Account
Prepaid expense	Prepaid insurance Prepaid rent	Insurance expense Rent expense	Asset/Expense
Accrued expense	Wages and salaries payable Rent payable Interest payable	Wages and salaries expense Rent expense Interest expense	Liability/Expense
Accrued revenue	Interest receivable Rent receivable	Interest revenue Rent revenue	Asset/Revenue
Unearned revenue	Unearned interest Unearned rent	Interest revenue Rent revenue	Liability/Revenue
Estimated items	Accumulated depreciation Allowance for doubtful accounts	Depreciation expense Bad debt expense	Contra-asset or liability/Expense
Inventory adjustment	Inventory	Cost of goods sold Purchases Purchases returns and allowances	Asset/Expense

7
Prepare Adjusted Trial Balance

All adjusting entries in the general journal must be posted to the worksheet. After posting all entries, the adjusting entries are combined with the unadjusted trial balance totals. The result is the adjusted trial balance. Both adjusting entries and the adjusted trial balance for Simple Example Company were shown in Figure 1-8.

Adjusting entries must also be posted to the general ledger. This can be done at the same time postings are made to the worksheet. For convenience, most companies wait until after financial statements are prepared to post adjustments to the general ledger.

FIGURE 1-10
Simple Example Company
Adjusting Entries
(Recorded in General Journal)
December 2013

	DATE	ACCOUNT NUMBER	ACCOUNT NAME	POST	DEBIT	CREDIT
(1)	12-31-13	711	Bad debt expense	✓	49	
		104	Allowance for doubtful accounts	✓		49
			To record 2013 provision for bad debts			
(2)	12-31-13	104	Allowance for doubtful accounts	✓	26	
		103	Accounts receivable	✓		26
			To write off uncollectible account receivable			
(3)	12-31-13	705	Rent expense	✓	4	
		106	Prepaid rent	✓		4
			To record December rent expense			
(4)	12-31-13	709	Depreciation expense	✓	15	
		202	Accumulated depreciation	✓		15
			To record 2013 depreciation			
(5)	12-31-13	712	Wages and salaries expense — admin.	✓	6	
		713	Wages and salaries expense — selling	✓	6	
		302	Wages and salaries payable	✓		12
			To record accrued payroll at 12-31-13			
(6)	12-31-13	715	Other payroll tax expense	✓	4	
		303	Payroll taxes payable	✓		4
			To accrue other payroll taxes at 12-31-13			
(7)	12-31-13	714	Employer's FICA expense	✓	5	
		306	FICA taxes payable	✓		5
			To accrue FICA taxes at 12-31-13			
(8)	12-31-13	703	Purchases discounts	✓	46	
		701	Cost of goods sold	✓	2,132	
		105	Inventory	✓		12
		702	Purchases	✓		2,166
			To adjust inventory (to reflect results of 12-31-13 physical count) and to record cost of goods sold			

The final step on the worksheet is completing the income statement and balance sheet columns. The information in these columns is used to prepare the financial statements.

As shown in the worksheet in Figure 1-8, the totals from the adjusted trial balance are transferred into either the income statement or balance sheet columns. In addition, the net loss is shown as a reduction in both the income statement debit column and the balance sheet credit column. If there had been net income for the year, the amounts would have been shown as increases in the same columns.

The financial statements are prepared directly from the income statement and balance sheet columns in the worksheet. There are several differences between the worksheet totals and the financial statements.

- The financial statements' descriptions and details must be carefully stated to conform to generally accepted accounting principles.

- Frequently, more than one account balance is combined in the trial balance to make up a financial statement total. For example, all selling expenses may be combined and only total selling expense included in the financial statements.

- Classified financial statements must distinguish between current and non-current assets and liabilities. Trial balances usually do not.

- Financial statements must include a cash flow statement. Some information to prepare that statement may or may not be available on the trial balance. Examples include proceeds from new loans and payments made on loans during the period.

- Footnote information and other disclosures required for financial statements are usually not available on the trial balance.

At the end of each year, all revenue and expense accounts are closed. Closing the accounts means eliminating the ending balance and starting with a zero balance in the next year.

The closing process happens only annually, even when monthly or quarterly statements are prepared. Many organizations use a calendar year for preparing annual statements. The closing process, therefore, occurs on December 31. Other companies choose different year-ends and thus close at different dates.

There are three closing entries for a typical company:

1. Close all revenue accounts to income summary. (Debit all revenue accounts and credit the income summary account.)

2. Close all expense accounts to income summary. (Debit income summary and credit expense accounts.)

3. Close the income summary to stockholders' equity.

For a sole proprietorship or partnership, the income summary is closed to one or more capital accounts. In a corporation it is closed to retained earnings.

Several facts about closing entries are important to understand:

- Closing entries are prepared only at the end of the organization's year. The year-end may be December 31 or another month-end.

- Closing entries are prepared after all transactions and adjusting entries have been prepared and posted to the general ledger. Closing entries complete the accounting process for the current period.

- Every revenue and expense account must be closed to enable the company to begin a new year with a zero balance.

- The total debits and total credits must be equal for each closing entry.

- Each account in each closing entry is posted individually to the appropriate general ledger account.

- Closing entries are recorded initially in the general journal and then posted to the general ledger.

Closing entries for Simple Example Company are shown in Figure 1-11. To avoid confusion when you study each cycle in Chapters 3 through 6, they have not yet been posted to the general ledger.

FIGURE 1-11
Simple Example Company
Closing Entries
(Recorded in General Journal)
December 2013

	DATE	ACCOUNT NUMBER	ACCOUNT NAME	POST	DEBIT	CREDIT
(1)	12-31-13	601	Sales	✓	3,648	
		603	Sales returns and allowances	✓		214
		604	Sales discounts taken	✓		182
		800	Income summary	✓		3,252
			To close revenue accounts to income summary			
(2)	12-31-13	800	Income summary	✓	3,313	
		701	Cost of goods sold	✓		2,132
		705	Rent expense	✓		48
		706	Repair expense	✓		69
		707	Utility expense	✓		62
		708	Postage expense	✓		49
		709	Depreciation expense	✓		15
		710	Travel expense	✓		57
		711	Bad debt expense	✓		49
		712	Wages and salaries expense - admin.	✓		270
		713	Wages and salaries expense - selling	✓		459
		714	Employer's FICA expense	✓		56
		715	Other payroll tax expense	✓		45
		717	Interest expense	✓		2
			To close expense accounts to income summary			
(3)	12-31-13	503	Retained earnings	✓	61	
		800	Income summary	✓		61
			To close income summary to retained earnings			

POST-CLOSING TRIAL BALANCE

After closing entries are posted to the general ledger, only balance sheet accounts will have balances. The amount in each balance sheet account, except retained earnings, should be the same as the amount in the adjusted trial balance. The balance in retained earnings should equal the ending balance in the statement of retained earnings.

Many accountants prepare a post-closing trial balance after all closing entries are posted.

The purposes are to make sure that debits equal credits in the general ledger before the recording process starts for the next year, the retained earnings balance is correct, and there are no balances in any income statement accounts.

The post-closing trial balance is a two-column listing, much like the first two columns in a worksheet. The source of each amount is the general ledger balance.

Figure 1-12 illustrates a post-closing trial balance for Simple Example Company at 12-31-13.

FIGURE 1-12
Simple Example Company
Post-Closing Trial Balance
December 31, 2013

	Account	Dr	Cr
101	Cash in bank	$ 78	
102	Payroll cash	5	
103	Accounts receivable	272	
104	Allowance for doubtful accounts		$ 41
105	Inventory	114	
106	Prepaid rent	4	
201	Delivery equipment	60	
202	Accumulated depreciation		60
301	Accounts payable		158
302	Wages and salaries payable		12
303	Payroll taxes payable		4
305	Withholding taxes payable		6
306	FICA taxes payable		10
501	Common stock		200
503	Retained earnings		42
		$533	$533

RELATIONSHIPS AMONG FINANCIAL STATEMENTS, TRIAL BALANCES, LEDGERS, JOURNALS, DOCUMENTS, AND TRANSACTIONS

To summarize the recording process, Figure 1-13 shows the relationships among financial statements, trial balances, ledgers, journals, documents, and transactions. The documents, journals, and ledgers are used to record transactions. Each of them is essential to the ultimate preparation of financial statements.

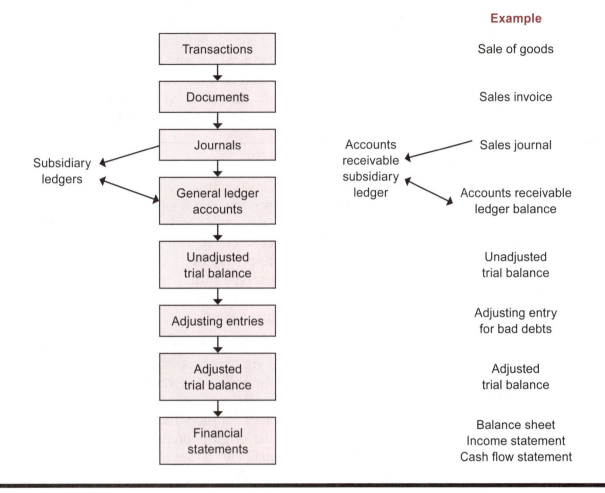

INTERNAL CONTROLS

Internal controls are the methods used by a company to safeguard its assets and provide reasonable assurance of the accuracy of accounting data. Most companies have internal controls at each stage of the accounting process.

The use of documents and records throughout a company is directly related to a company's internal controls. The following are the primary types of controls that need to be understood for the *Systems Understanding Aid.*

Adequate documents and records. The appropriate design and control of documents and records improves the likelihood of the correct transmission of information to users. Certain principles dictate their design and use. Documents and records should be:

- Prenumbered consecutively. This helps determine whether documents are missing and helps locate documents when they are needed at a later date.

- Prepared before a transaction occurs, at the time it occurs, or as soon thereafter as possible. When there is a long time interval, the chance for error increases.

- Sufficiently simple to make sure that they are clearly understood.

- Designed for multiple uses whenever possible. This minimizes the number of different forms required. For example, a properly designed sales invoice can

25

be the basis for recording sales in the journals, the authority for shipment, the basis for developing sales statistics, and the support for sales commissions.

- Constructed in a manner that aids in correct preparation. For example, a document might include blank spaces for authorization and designated column spaces for numerical data.

Authorization of transactions. Every transaction must be properly authorized if control is to be satisfactory. If any person in an organization could acquire or expend assets at will, the undesirable lack of control should be evident. An example of authorization is the approval of credit by the credit manager.

The person authorizing a transaction frequently signs or initials the document to communicate the authorization to subsequent users of the document. For example, the credit manager might initial the customer purchase order to show the shipping department that credit has been approved and shipment is therefore appropriate.

Separation of the custody of assets from accounting. The reason for not permitting a person who has temporary or permanent custody of an asset to account for that asset is to protect the company against fraud. When one person performs both functions, there is an excessive risk of the asset being disposed of for personal gain and the records adjusted to relieve the person of responsibility for the asset. If the cashier, for example, receives cash and maintains both the cash and accounts receivable records, it is possible for the person to take the cash received from a customer and adjust the customer's account by failing to record a sale or by recording a fictitious credit.

Independent checks on performance. An independent check on performance is a review of transactions and related assets for propriety and correct recording by a person not originally responsible for any aspect of the transactions. The purpose of independent checks is to make sure record keeping is done accurately, completely, and honestly.

It is important for a different person to perform the checks than those originally responsible for doing the recording or handling related assets. The one doing the checking should also not be a subordinate, relative, or close friend of the original preparer if independence is to be maintained. Several types of independent checks are shown below.

Common Types of Independent Checks	Examples
Recalculations	Re-extend a sales invoice (price times quantity).
Reconciliations	Prepare a bank reconciliation.
Number sequencing	Account for a sequence of duplicate sales invoice numbers.
Comparisons	Compare total quantities on a duplicate sales invoice to quantities on the customer purchase order.

The performance of independent checks is frequently indicated on documents or records by initialing them. For example, after an employee has re-extended the sales invoice, the document would be initialed by that employee. Even though initialing a document for approval and initialing it for internal verification have the same appearance, they perform different functions.

Documents and records play an important role in a company's control environment. Since the design, maintenance, and day-to-day functioning of adequate internal controls are the responsibility of the management of a company, management should be aware of the internal control aspects of documents and records.

CHAPTER 2

Flowcharting

This chapter covers the preparation and proper use of flowcharts and narratives. Background information about the need for documentation of accounting systems and the use of narratives is also included.

NEED FOR A WRITTEN DESCRIPTION OF A CLIENT'S ACCOUNTING SYSTEM

A written description of the accounting system affecting a company's financial statements serves several purposes:

- Minimizes the likelihood of an incomplete or ineffective accounting system. The description is an inexpensive way to describe the system before the system is developed.

- Provides a record for training new employees and reminding existing personnel how the system should operate.

- Assists in making improvements to the system. An accurate description of the system will enable personnel to analyze it and suggest improvement.

- Provides information for accounting personnel to communicate with other personnel about the system. For example, if sales personnel do not understand how or why an existing system is used, the description can be used to illustrate the system.

- Improves the ability to communicate with people outside the company. For example, independent CPAs are required to have a complete understanding of a company's accounting system. Frequently they use the client's description rather than developing their own.

To obtain maximum benefit from a description of an accounting system, it should describe the following five items:

1. The origin of every document and record in the system. For example, the description should state how orders are received from customers and how sales invoices arise. There is an exception to this guideline for subsidiary and general ledgers and journals. Their source and disposition need not be indicated.

2. All processing that takes place. For example, if a customer purchase order is attached to a copy of the sales invoice, that should be described.

3. The disposition of every document and record in the system. The filing of documents, sending them to customers, or destroying them should be shown.

4. The department or personnel performing the duties.

5. The existing internal controls. These controls typically include:

   - separation of duties (e.g., recording of cash separated from handling cash).

   - authorizations and approvals (e.g., credit approval).

   - independent checks (e.g., recalculation of extensions on a sales invoice).

NARRATIVE DESCRIPTIONS

Narratives are written descriptions of a company's accounting system. The disadvantage of a narrative is the difficulty of describing a system in a sufficiently clear and simple manner.

Frequently narratives omit certain parts of the system and thereby increase the chance of misunderstanding the system. For example, some narratives fail to indicate internal controls or departments doing the tasks.

The use of a narrative is common when a system is simple and easy to describe. It is always acceptable to use a narrative if it is understandable and if it includes the five items previously described.

FLOWCHARTS

A flowchart is a diagram that graphically shows a company's documents and records and their sequential flow in the organization. There are three common types of flowcharts:

1. **Systems flowchart.** This type of flowchart emphasizes the flow of documents and records in the organization. It does not show the segregation of duties. The advantage of not showing the segregation of duties is that it makes the flowchart easier to understand. Most companies believe that showing the segregation of duties is important; therefore, systems flowcharts are usually not used for accounting or auditing purposes.

2. **Internal control flowchart.** The difference between systems and internal control flowcharts is that the latter shows the segregation of duties, plus other internal controls. Everything included in a systems flowchart is also included on the internal control flowchart. The disadvantage of showing the segregation of duties and other controls is the difficulty of preparing and reading the flowchart, especially when one person in the entity performs more than one function. Most companies believe the segregation of duties and other controls are sufficiently important to justify the additional complexity. The authors recommend the use of internal control flowcharts.

3. **Program flowchart.** This flowchart is more detailed than the previous two. Its primary use is for computer programming. Segregation of duties is not shown in a program flowchart. These flowcharts are usually used only by computer programmers and other computer specialists.

FLOWCHARTING SYMBOLS

Symbols are used to show predefined items, steps, and actions. No matter what symbols are used, the concept of flowcharting remains unchanged, but naturally the symbols must be defined. Different companies use different symbols, but most of them have been derived from the United States of America Standards Institute symbols and are similar in form. Figure 2-1 (page 30) shows the symbols that have been adopted for this text and gives an example of each symbol.

FLOWCHARTING TECHNIQUES

Flowcharts communicate the flow of documents and records and also internal controls. There are several qualities that help flowcharts communicate effectively:

- **Use of specialized symbols.** These are shown in Figure 2-1.

- **Use of flowlines.** In preparing flowcharts, flowlines should cross as infrequently as possible.

Flowlines are used to show how documents and records are related. Arrowheads are used to indicate the direction of the flow. Many flowcharters follow the convention that arrowheads are used only for flowlines upward and to the left. Wherever there are no arrowheads, the reader knows the flowlines read downward or to the right. We recommend using arrowheads whenever it adds clarification. Throughout both the Reference and the Project, arrows are used for all flows.

A distinction is made at the bottom of Figure 2-1 between using a solid line and a dotted one. When a solid line is used, the document or record goes to the place indicated. A dotted line is used to show that information from the document or record is used in either a process or another document or record.

A typical example of the use of a dotted flowline is shown in Figure 2-2 (page 31) for posting to the employee earnings subsidiary ledger and payroll journal. This information on the weekly payroll summary is used to update the time records, but the document does not actually flow there.

- **Show separation of duties.** Areas of responsibility are established on flowcharts as vertical columns or horizontal rows. This technique enables the reader to clearly identify changes in responsibility as the documents flow through the system. An example of separation of duties by areas of responsibility is given in Figure 2-2.

- **Include relevant internal controls.** The inclusion of significant internal controls in a flowchart aids the company in evaluating the adequacy of internal controls. Examples include authorizations, independent checks, and reconciliations. Figure 2-2 includes several internal controls in the flowchart.

- **Include written comments and clarification.** The use of comments and explanations is encouraged whenever it helps make a flowchart more complete or easier to understand. There are two types of written comments: annotations and footnotes. Annotations are indicated by an open-sided rectangle and are included within the flowchart. Footnotes are included at the bottom or on one side. Annotation is preferred when there is sufficient room in the flowchart. Frequently internal controls can be identified most effectively by written comments. Annotations and footnotes are both demonstrated in Figure 2-2.

- **Show the source of every document in the flowchart.** Every document must come from one of three sources: (1) received from a source outside the company, (2) received from a department not shown in the flowchart, or (3) prepared by a department included in the flowchart.

- **Use a process symbol for every document or record prepared.** Every document must result from some type of action, such as preparing a payroll check. The action should be shown by use of a process symbol.

- **Show the disposition of every document in the flowchart.** Every document must go to one of three places: (1) sent to a source outside the company, (2) sent to a department not shown in the flowchart, or (3) filed.

Notice in Figure 2-2 that the source and disposition of all documents are shown. Financial records, such as the employee earnings subsidiary ledger and the payroll journal, exist within the function being flowcharted. Therefore, they do not flow anywhere and their source and disposition need not be shown.

FIGURE 2-1
Flowcharting Symbols for Manual Systems

Document — paper documents and reports of all types. *Examples:* sales invoice, receiving report, time card.

Manual Operation or Process — the performance by a human of any processing function which causes a change in value, form, or location of information. *Example:* sales invoice prepared by clerk.

Terminal — beginning, ending, or interruption of flowchart; used to indicate information entering or leaving system. *Example:* receipt of order from customer.

Off-line Storage — off-line storage of documents and records. *Example:* a duplicate sales invoice is filed in numerical order (typically N-numerical, A-alphabetical, D-date, T-temporary).

Journal/Ledger Symbol — recording of processed information in journals/ledgers. *Example:* entry in sales journal.

Decision — used to indicate a decision requiring different actions for a yes or no answer. *Example:* Is customer credit satisfactory?

Annotation — the addition of descriptive comments or explanatory notes as clarification. *Example:* a billing clerk checks credit before preparing an invoice.

On-page Connector — exit to, or entry from, another part of flowchart on <u>same page</u>; keyed by using numbers. *Example:* a document transfer from one department to another.

Off-page Connector — exit to, or entry from, another part of flowchart on <u>different page</u>; keyed by using page numbers and key letters. *Example:* flowchart logic jumps to page four (4), key letter B.

Directional Flowlines
1. Direction of processing or data flow
2. Dotted line indicates only information flow, not document flow.

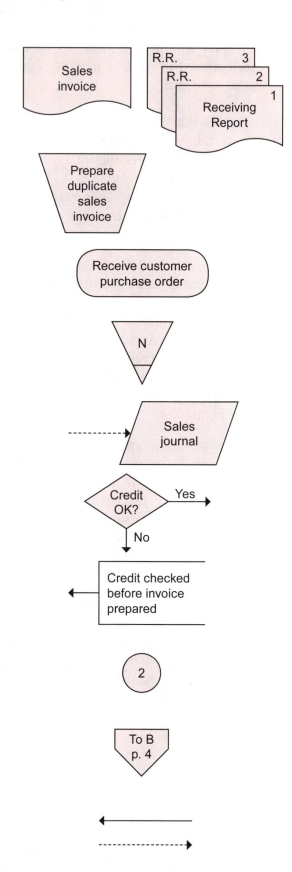

FIGURE 2-2
Flowchart Illustrating Separation of Duties and Internal Controls (Payroll Transactions Cycle)

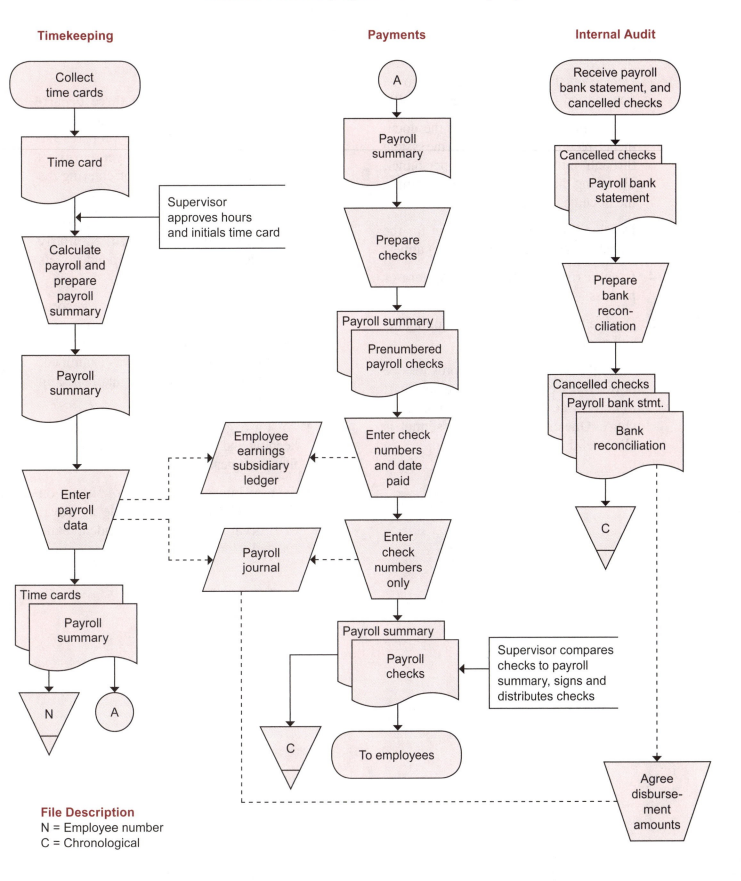

File Description
N = Employee number
C = Chronological

OVERALL APPROACH

Incorporating the above flowcharting techniques should result in readable and relevant flowcharts. The following are steps ordinarily followed in preparing flowcharts:

1. Decide on the system or process to be flowcharted (purchasing, sales, payroll).

2. Determine information about the documents, records, and activities in the system through interviewing client personnel, observing their activities, and examining the documents and records.

3. Develop a tentative organization for the flowchart including segregation of duties.

4. Draw a rough sketch of the system or process.

5. Draw a flowchart, including comments and annotations.

6. Trace the documents and records for one or two transactions through the flowchart to determine the accuracy of the flowchart. Questioning client personnel is also useful at this point.

SUMMARY

The purpose of the flowchart is to graphically show a company's documents and records and their sequential flow, including internal controls. The following observations about the flowchart in Figure 2-2 summarize the chapter.

- The flowchart shows the three departments involved in payroll. Notice, for example, that Timekeeping prepares the payroll journal and employee earnings subsidiary ledger, except for entering the check number and date paid.

- Every document can be traced to where it was received or prepared. Similarly each document can be traced to its disposition.

- Solid lines mean documents or records were prepared, filed, or distributed. Dotted lines mean that information on the documents or records was examined. Annotations explain what happened in certain steps.

- An on-page connector between Timekeeping and Payments is used to keep the flowchart neat.

- Several internal controls are shown on the flowchart. These include approval of timecards and an independent bank reconciliation.

CHAPTER 3

Sales and Cash Receipts Cycle

This chapter discusses the transactions, documents, and records for sales and cash receipts. First an overview is provided for each of the five subcycles of the overall cycle. The remainder of the chapter covers the actions in each subcycle and the transactions resulting from those actions.

The sales and cash receipts cycle starts with the receipt of an order from a customer for goods or services and ends with the collection and recording of the cash receipt for the sale. An essential part of the cycle is the recording of accounts receivable.

SUBCYCLES, ACTIONS, COMMON TRANSACTIONS, AND TYPICAL ACCOUNTS AFFECTED

There are five primary subcycles in the sales and cash receipts cycle. Several actions take place for each subcycle. The recording of these actions results in transactions, which in turn result in changes in account balances. The five subcycles are shown below.

Subcycles	Actions	Common Transactions	Typical Account Balances Affected
Sales	Receive orders from customers, ship goods, bill customers, record sales in journal and subsidiary ledger, summarize journal and post to general ledger.	Cash sales Credit sales	Sales Cash Accounts receivable
Cash receipts	Receive cash, enter in cash receipts prelist, deposit cash, record cash receipts in journal and subsidiary ledger, summarize journal and post to general ledger.	Collections on accounts receivable Loans Collections on loans receivable Cash sales Sale of fixed assets or securities	Cash Accounts receivable Notes payable Sales discounts taken Gain or loss on the sale of assets Sales
Sales returns and allowances	Process sales returns and allowances requests, receive goods (returns only), credit customers, record in journal and subsidiary ledger, summarize journal and post to general ledger.	Sales returns Sales allowances	Accounts receivable Sales returns and allowances
Estimate of bad debt expense	Determine provision for bad debts, record in general journal and post to general ledger.	Bad debt provision	Bad debt expense* Allowance for doubtful accounts*
Write-off of uncollectible accounts	Identify uncollectible accounts receivable, record in general journal, post to subsidiary ledger and to general ledger.	Uncollectible accounts written off	Accounts receivable* Allowance for doubtful accounts*

*Assumes the use of the allowance method for recording uncollectible accounts receivable.

ACCOUNTANT'S OBJECTIVES

The accountant's objectives in recording transactions in the sales and cash receipts cycle and summarizing the resultant account balances include the following:

1. All existing transactions for each subcycle are recorded.

2. All transactions are recorded and summarized at the correct amounts.

3. All transactions are correctly classified as defined by the chart of accounts.

4. All transactions are included in the proper period.

5. Uncollectible receivables at the balance sheet date are written off.

6. The valuation of the allowance for doubtful accounts is reasonable at the balance sheet date.

7. All material disclosures affecting the accounts are included in the financial statements and related footnotes.

SALES — ACTIONS AND RELATED DOCUMENTS

Figure 3-1 includes a flowchart of the actions and related documents for sales in a typical company. Discussion of the information in the flowchart follows.

FIGURE 3-1
Sales — Actions and Related Documents

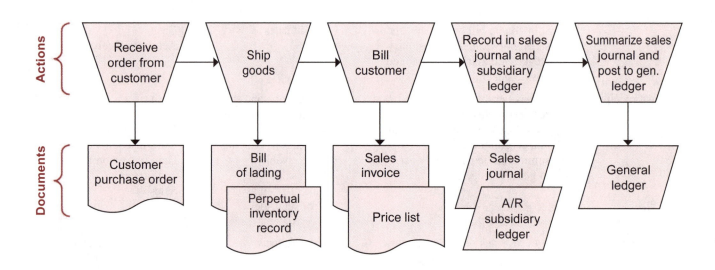

ACTIONS	DOCUMENTS
Receive order from customer — Receipt of an order from a customer for goods is the starting point for a sale. The order may be a document or an order can be prepared by a salesperson or receptionist taking orders over the phone or in person.	**Customer purchase order** — A document prepared to request goods or services from a customer. The form should include the name and address of the customer, goods or services desired, and the desired delivery or performance date.
Ship goods or perform services — In most cases, generally accepted accounting principles require the recognition of a revenue and the transaction recorded as of the date when the goods were shipped or services performed. The shipment of goods or performance of services is therefore an essential function in accounting. In some systems, a shipping document is prepared as a by-product of billing customers. In these systems, billing precedes shipping.	**Bill of lading or other shipping document** — A document prepared at the time of shipment indicating the description of the merchandise, the quantity shipped, and other relevant data. A bill of lading is a written contract of the receipt and shipment of goods between the seller and the carrier. It must be used when a common carrier (shipper registered with the Interstate Commerce Commission) ships the goods. A different type of shipping document is used when a company ships its own goods, but the document's function is the same. Ordinarily, bills of lading and other shipping documents do not include dollar values. Figure 3-2 (page 36) shows an example of a completed bill of lading for the shipment of goods sold by Simple Example Company. In this example, the freight is being charged to the seller.
Bill customer — Billing is the means by which the customer is informed of the amount that is owed for the merchandise shipped. The proper amount of the bill depends on the quantity shipped and the price charged. The billing must also recognize freight charges, insurance, and terms of payment.	**Sales invoice** — A document prepared indicating the description and quantity of goods sold, the price including freight, insurance, terms, other relevant data, and the total amount of the sale. It is the method of indicating to the customer the amount of a sale and due date of a payment. The original is sent to a customer and one or more copies are retained. It is also the document used for recording sales in the accounting records.
	Price List — A list prepared by the company indicating product prices for billings. It is usually developed by marketing personnel and approved by management.

FIGURE 3-2
Example of a Typical Bill of Lading

UNIFORM STRAIGHT BILL OF LADING — **Domestic**

Simple Example Company
19100 Stewart Avenue
Battle Creek, Michigan 49015
(616) 555-2600

Shipper No. **138694**
Carrier No. **5439**
Date **11-17-13**

TO:

Consignee **Taylor Products**

Street **5005 Territorial Boulevard**

City/State **East Lansing, MI**   Zip Code **48826**

Baldwin Trucking Company
(Name of Carrier)

Route **Express**   Vehicle Number **XY 2497**

No. Shipping Units	Kind of Packaging, Description of Articles, Special Marks and Exceptions			Weight (Subject to Correction)	Rate	Charges (for Carrier use only)
4	Cartons	UB734	Frames	124 lb.	$6.00/100 lb.	7.44
2	Cartons	TX201	Photo Albums	113 lb.	$6.00/100 lb.	6.78
6	Cartons	DF844	Digital Cameras	225 lb.	$6.00/100 lb.	13.50
1	Carton	VJ693	Scanners	70 lb.	$6.00/100 lb.	4.20

REMIT C.O.D. TO:

ADDRESS **N/A**

COD Amt: $ **N/A**

C.O.D. FEE:
PREPAID ☐ $
COLLECT ☐   **N/A**

Note — Where the rate is dependent on value, shippers are required to state specifically in writing the agreed or declared value of the property.
The agreed or declared value of the property is hereby specifically stated by the shipper to be not exceeding.

$ **N/A** per **N/A**

Subject to Section 7 of the conditions, if this shipment is to be delivered to the consignee without recourse on the consignor, the consignor shall sign the following statement:
The carrier shall not make delivery of this shipment without payment of freight and all other lawful charges.

N/A
(Signature of Consignor)

Total Charges $ **31.92**

FREIGHT CHARGES
Check Appropriate Box:
☐ **Freight Prepaid**   ☐ **Collect**
☒ **Bill to Shipper**

Received subject to the classifications and tariffs in effect on the date of the issue of this Bill of Lading, the property described above in apparent good order, except as noted (contents and condition of contents of packages unknown), marked, consigned, and destined as indicated above which said carrier (the word carrier being understood throughout this contract as meaning any person or corporation in possession of the property under the contract) agrees to carry to its usual place of delivery at said destination, if on its route, otherwise to deliver to another carrier on the route to said destination. It is mutually agreed as to each carrier of all or any of, said property over all or any portion of said route to destination and as to each party at any time interested in all or any said property, that every service to be performed hereunder shall be to all the bill of lading terms and conditions in the governing classification on the date of shipment.

Shipper hereby certifies that he is familiar with all the bill of lading terms and conditions in the governing classification and the said terms and conditions are hereby agreed to by the shipper and accepted for himself and his assigns.

SHIPPER	**Simple Example Company**	CARRIER	**Baldwin Trucking**	
PER	**Simple Example's Employee**	PER	**Joe Driver**	DATE **11-17-13**

(This Bill of Lading is to be signed by the shipper and agent of the carrier issuing same.)

ACTIONS	DOCUMENTS
Record in sales journal and subsidiary ledger — The sales journal is the record of original entry for sales transactions. Every sales transaction must be recorded in the sales journal, individually or in summary form. (Some companies record cash sales in the cash receipts journal.) Every credit sale must also be recorded in the accounts receivable subsidiary ledger as an increase in a customer's account receivable balance.	**Sales journal** — A journal for recording sales. It usually indicates gross sales for different classifications, such as product lines, the entry to accounts receivable, and miscellaneous debits and credits. Some companies include only daily summaries in the journals. Copies of each day's duplicate sales invoices are retained, and these copies are totaled to equal the total sales recorded in the journal. Totals of details in the journal are typically posted to the general ledger monthly.
	Accounts receivable subsidiary ledger — A ledger for recording individual sales, cash receipts, and sales returns and allowances for each customer. The total of the individual account balances in the subsidiary ledger equals the total balance of accounts receivable in the general ledger.
Summarize sales journal and post to general ledger — Periodically, usually monthly, the sales journal is totaled. The totals are then transferred (posted) to the general ledger. When all sales are on account, it is common to have only one column for sales in the sales journal. The total for the month is then posted to both accounts receivable (debit) and sales (credit) in the general ledger. There may also be separate columns for sales to employees, cash sales, trade discounts, and sales returns and allowances.	**General ledger** — A record used to summarize transactions recorded in the journals. For sales, every account included in the sales journal (e.g., sales, accounts receivable and sales discounts taken) must also be included in the general ledger. Only the totals in the sales journal are posted to the general ledger.

After a billing is made to a customer, including the recording of the receivable, there are three ways the receivable can be eliminated: collection of cash, sales return and allowance, or write-off as uncollectible. An accounting system must provide for all three. Rather than being thought of as independent, these three ways should be thought of as being related to sales.

CASH RECEIPTS — ACTIONS AND RELATED DOCUMENTS

For most companies, it is convenient to categorize cash receipts in three ways: collections on accounts receivable, cash sales, and "all others." The "all others" category includes cash receipts from such things as borrowing, sales of or interest on investments, and disposal of fixed assets.

Some companies choose to record all cash receipts in a cash receipts journal. Others choose to record both cash and account sales in the sales journal; therefore, only collections and "all others" are included in the cash receipts journal. Either method is satisfactory as long as the accounting records are accurate and cash is properly controlled.

The actions and related documents for a typical company's cash receipts subcycle are shown in Figure 3-3 (page 38). More detailed discussion of the information in Figure 3-3 follows.

FIGURE 3-3
Cash Receipts — Actions and Related Documents

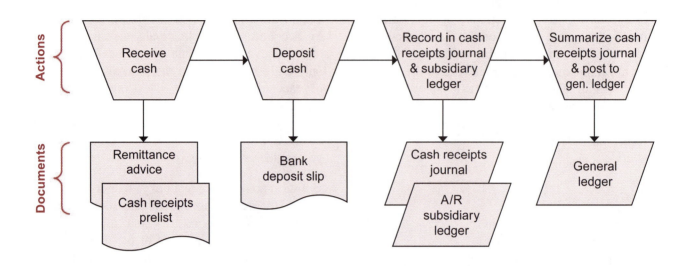

ACTIONS	DOCUMENTS
Receive cash — The starting point for recording cash, regardless of its source, is its receipt. Generally accepted accounting principles require there cognition of cash as an asset at the receipt date rather than the date of deposit or date of mailing by the sender.	**Remittance advice** — A document that accompanies the sales invoice mailed to the customer and can be returned to the seller with the cash payment. It is used to indicate the customer name, the sales invoice number, and the amount of the invoice when the payment is received. The primary purpose of a remittance advice is to make sure that the proper customer is credited for the proper amount of cash received. Companies whose cash receipts are easily associated with specific sales transactions often do not use remittance advices.
	The remittance advice can be an extra copy of the sales invoice sent to the customer with the original. The extra copy would probably be stamped "Please return this copy with your payment." When a remittance advice is not returned by the customer, a clerk will prepare one. Remittance advices facilitate the immediate deposit of the cash.
	When customers pay on the basis of monthly statements, rather than individual invoices (such as for gasoline credit cards), the remittance advice is for the total balance due rather than an individual invoice.
	(continued on following page)

ACTIONS	DOCUMENTS
	Cash receipts prelist — A list prepared when cash is received, which lists each cash receipt. This document is used later to verify whether cash received was recorded and deposited at the correct amounts and on a timely basis.
Deposit cash — Cash should be deposited in the bank as quickly as is practical, usually daily. The reasons are to make it available for company use and to reduce the likelihood of accidental loss or theft.	**Bank deposit slip** — A document prepared to accompany bank deposits, which lists each check and all currency being deposited. A separate bank deposit slip is prepared for each deposit. Usually banks require one to reduce the likelihood of bank errors. They are also helpful in recording cash receipts and preparing bank reconciliations. Deposit slips are especially helpful when company or bank personnel have made an error. The bank usually indicates the amount of the deposit on the deposit slip by use of a cash register. The bank keeps the original and returns a validated copy to the depositor.
Record in cash receipts journal and subsidiary ledger — The cash receipts journal is the record of original entry for cash receipts transactions. It should look almost the same as the sales journal except for differences in the account titles. The subsidiary ledger is the same record described as a part of sales.	**Cash receipts journal** — A journal for recording cash receipts from collections, cash sales, and all other cash receipts. It indicates total cash received, the credit to accounts receivable at the gross amount of the original sale, sales discounts taken, and other debits and credits. The daily entries in the cash receipts journal are supported by remittance advices. The accountant must use care in recording the credit to accounts receivable in the cash receipts journal so that it is consistent with the recording of the original sale. Assume, for example, a sale for $100 with a 2% cash discount allowed. If the receivable was originally recorded at $100 and $98 cash was received, the credit to accounts receivable in the cash receipts journal must be $100, not $98, if the discount was granted. The credit to accounts receivable in the subsidiary ledger must also be for $100, not $98. The $2 discount is recorded as a debit to the sales discounts taken account. **Accounts receivable subsidiary ledger** — See Sales (page 37).
Summarize cash receipts journal and post to general ledger — The concepts are the same for this action as for sales and are not repeated.	**General ledger** — See Sales (page 37).

SALES RETURNS AND ALLOWANCES — ACTIONS AND RELATED DOCUMENTS

Sales returns are the returns of merchandise to the seller for such reasons as the incorrect product being sent, defective merchandise, and the customer no longer needing the goods. For sales allowances, the customer keeps the goods purchased but is granted a reduction in the selling price.

The actions and recording of sales returns and allowances are nearly the same as for sales, but instead of a bill to the customer, a credit is granted. A major difference between sales and sales returns and allowances is that sales returns and allowances are often immaterial.

Figure 3-4 shows the actions and related documents for sales returns and allowances business activity. More detailed discussion of the activities and information in Figure 3-4 follows.

FIGURE 3-4
Sales Returns and Allowances — Actions and Related Documents

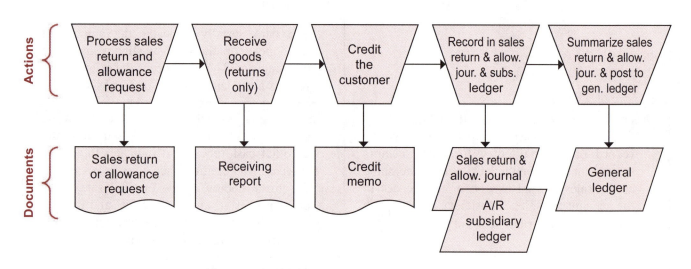

ACTIONS	DOCUMENTS
Process sales return and allowance request — Receipt of a request from a customer to return goods or for an allowance is the starting point for recording the sales return or allowance. Typically, it is approved by a salesperson or sales manager. It is common for the parties to negotiate the amount of the credit.	**Sales return request —** A document requesting authority to return goods. A document is not normally used for allowances. Figure 3-5 (page 42) shows an example of a sales return request received from one of Simple Example Company's customers, Taylor Products. When the sales return request was received from Taylor Products, the last four columns were blank. The handwritten information in these columns was completed by Simple Example Company when the returned goods were received from Taylor Products. This information is later used to prepare a credit memo for the sales return transaction. Credit memos are discussed shortly.

ACTIONS	DOCUMENTS
Receive goods (returns only) — Generally accepted accounting principles require the recognition of sales returns and allowances in the same accounting period that the original sale was made, rather than the period of the actual receipt of the goods. For convenience, many companies recognize returns when the goods are actually received back from customers. An adjustment can be made later for material returns.	**Receiving report** — A document prepared at the time the goods are received showing the description of the goods received, quantity and date received. This document serves the same function as a shipping document. Receiving reports are discussed more fully in Chapter 4 as part of the purchases and cash disbursements cycle.
Credit the customer — The credit to the customer performs the same function as billing—to inform the customer of the amount of the credit. It is important in issuing credits for returns and allowances to have agreement from the customer on the amount of the credit. It is not always for the full amount of the sale, even for returned goods.	**Credit memo** — A document prepared indicating the amount and terms of the return or allowance. The original is sent to the customer and one or more copies are retained. It is also the document used for recording sales returns and allowances in the accounting records.
Record in sales returns and allowances journal and subsidiary ledger — The sales returns and allowances journal is the record of original entry for both sales returns and allowances. It can be a separate journal or a part of the sales journal.	**Sales returns and allowances journal** — A journal for recording sales returns and allowances. Many companies record returns and allowances in the sales journal. If they are recorded in the sales journal, a separate column is used. A separate journal is used only when there are many sales returns and allowances transactions. **Accounts receivable subsidiary ledger** — See Sales (page 37).
Summarize sales returns and allowances journal and post to general ledger — The concepts are the same for this action as for sales and are not repeated.	**General ledger** — See Sales (page 37).

FIGURE 3-5
Example of a Sales Return Request

REQUEST TO RETURN FROM →

Vendor:

Taylor Products
5005 Territorial Boulevard
East Lansing, Michigan 48826

Ret. Request No. 3498

Date of Request   11-29-13

SIMPLE EXAMPLE COMPANY
19100 Stewart Avenue
Battle Creek, Michigan 49015

All returns will be clean, in saleable condition, and shipped prepaid. A prompt reply will be greatly appreciated. Thank you for your cooperation.

For Clarification Contact

Name   Sue Hinske

Phone   (517) 222-7900

RETURN CODES:

A Overstock   D Wrong product billed & shipped
B Damaged   E Correct product billed but wrong
C Defective   product shipped
           F Other

☐ Cash Refund - Please
☒ Credit to Account - Please

Account No.   1008
Request by   CJA

DEPT.	QUAN. REQ.	PRODUCT NUMBER	DESCRIPTION	RETURN CODE	INVOICE NO.	INVOICE DATE	QUAN. RET.	LIST PRICE	COST OR DISC.	EXTENSION
	10	TX201	Photo Album	A	138	11-17-13	10	7.95	—	79.50
	5	DF844	Digital Camera	A	138	11-17-13	5	129.75	—	648.75
							TOTAL			728.25

Simple Example's Employee   12-1-13

Return Authorized by   **Date**

ESTIMATE OF BAD DEBT EXPENSE — ACTIONS AND RELATED DOCUMENTS

Generally accepted accounting principles require accountants to recognize the expense for an uncollectible account receivable in the same period that the sale is made rather than when the account becomes uncollectible. Accountants usually recognize the expense by estimating bad debt expense periodically as a fixed percent of gross or net sales, based on historical experience. The debit is to bad debt expense and the credit to allowance for doubtful accounts. The actions and related documents for the periodic bad debt expense recognition are shown in Figure 3-6. Detailed discussion of Figure 3-6 follows.

FIGURE 3-6
Estimate of Bad Debt Expense — Actions and Related Documents

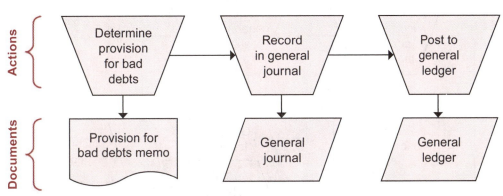

ACTIONS	DOCUMENTS
Determine provision for bad debts — When financial statements are prepared, the periodic provision for bad debts is determined. For example, if 2% of a company's net sales have historically not been collectible and net sales were $10,000 for the period, the amount of bad debt expense would be $200. The amount would be larger or smaller if there was reason to believe that the estimate does not reflect actual bad debt losses.	**Provision for bad debts memo** — A document indicating the amount of bad debts for a period. Many companies do not prepare this document. Alternatively, the explanation of the calculation can be shown in the general journal. A separate file is usually maintained showing the basis on which the periodic adjustment is made.
Record in general journal — The general journal is the journal of original entry for bad debt expense. The entry is recorded as a debit to bad debt expense and a credit to allowance for doubtful accounts.	**General journal** — A document for recording transactions not recorded in specialized journals. Transactions such as bad debt expense, where there is only one transaction for each month, are recorded in the general journal. The journal has two columns, one for debits and a second for credits.
Post to general ledger — There are no totals in the general journal to summarize before posting. Each transaction in the general journal is posted individually to the general ledger.	**General ledger** — See Sales (page 37).

WRITE-OFF OF UNCOLLECTIBLE ACCOUNTS RECEIVABLE — ACTIONS AND RELATED DOCUMENTS

In this subcycle, individual accounts that are no longer collectible are written off. The accounting entry to reflect the write-off is to debit the allowance for doubtful accounts and credit accounts receivable. The actions and related documents are shown in Figure 3-7. Detailed discussion follows.

FIGURE 3-7
Write-off of Uncollectible Accounts Receivable — Actions and Related Documents

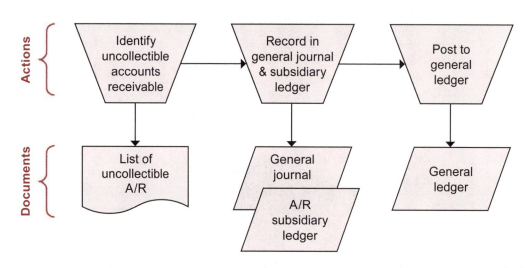

ACTIONS	DOCUMENTS
Identify uncollectible accounts receivable — Identifying of individual accounts receivable that are considered uncollectible is usually done by the credit manager. Frequently the accounts are considered uncollectible when a customer files bankruptcy, moves without a forwarding address, or when the account is turned over to a collection agency.	**List of uncollectible accounts receivable** — A prepared list that identifies accounts receivable that are not likely to be collected. The list is usually prepared periodically, such as monthly.
Record in general journal and subsidiary ledger — The general journal is the journal of original entry for the write-off of uncollectible accounts receivable. The periodic entry is a debit to allowance for doubtful accounts and a credit to accounts receivable in the amount of the total on the list of uncollectible receivables. The subsidiary ledger is credited for customers included on the list of uncollectible accounts receivable, in the amounts listed.	**General journal** — The journal used for the write-off of uncollectible accounts receivable. **Accounts receivable subsidiary ledger** — See Sales (page 37).
Post to general ledger — See estimate of bad debt cycle.	**General ledger** — See Sales (page 37).

ACCOUNTS RECEIVABLE AGED TRIAL BALANCE

An accounts receivable aged trial balance is a listing of the ending balances in the subsidiary accounts receivable ledger at a specific point in time. It includes a column for individual account balances and separate columns showing a breakdown of each balance by the time passed between the date of sale and the balance sheet date. An illustration of a typical accounts receivable aged trial balance is shown in Figure 3-8.

FIGURE 3-8
Accounts Receivable Aged Trial Balance Example

Anycompany, Inc.
Accounts Receivable Aged Trial Balance
November 30, 2013

Customer Number	Customer	Amount Due	Age in days			
			Current	31–60	61–90	Over 90
2130	James Abel	$ 342				$ 342
2131	Robert Bock	618	$ 318	$ 300		
2132	Timothy Chazen	1,340		1,300	$ 40	
2133	Oscar Darwin	6,290	6,000	290		
3134	Juliet Embry	3,412	2,000	1,012		400
3135	George Fain	141	141			
3136	Gayle Gershin	3,300	2,604	696		
3137	Andrew Hart	2,834	2,834			
2138	Terron Ismael	(928)	(928)			
	Totals	$ 17,349	$ 12,969	$ 3,598	$ 40	$ 742

The accounts receivable aged trial balance fulfills three purposes for a company:

1. Reconciles the control account to the subsidiary ledger as a check on certain recording errors. Examples of errors that will cause the trial balance not to reconcile with the control account include:

   • recording an account receivable at a different amount in the sales journal than in the subsidiary ledger.

   • incorrectly adding the accounts receivable column in the cash receipts journal.

   • incorrectly adding or subtracting amounts in the subsidiary ledger.

2. Shows a listing of accounts receivable in a convenient format to enable management to review the amount each customer owes. The aging is useful information to help management decide when and where greater collection effort is needed.

3. Provides information about the adequacy of the allowance for doubtful accounts and the need to write off certain accounts as uncollectible.

In preparing an accounts receivable aged trial balance, the accountant obtains the information directly from the subsidiary ledger as of a given balance sheet date. Each line on the accounts receivable aged trial balance is taken from the subsidiary ledger for one customer. The information on the line includes:

1. Customer number and name.

2. Total balance due from the customer. In some cases, the balance may be a credit. An example is when a customer has received a credit for returned goods after the receivable has been paid.

3. Aging. The aging is determined on the basis of the date of any sale for which collection has not been made. Usually the date for sales and cash receipts is indicated in the subsidiary ledger. Ordinarily, cash receipts are assumed to apply to the oldest outstanding receivables. For example, assume a November sale in the amount of $400, a December sale in the amount of $300, and December collection of $500. The remaining receivable of $200 is assumed to be for the December sale unless there is a dispute over the November sale.

INTERNAL CONTROLS

Chapter 1 includes a general introduction of internal controls affecting all cycles. The purpose of this section is to examine specific controls for the sales and cash receipts cycle. The most important controls for the cycle follow.

Adequate documents and records. The documents used in sales, sales returns and allowances, and cash receipts transactions should be prenumbered and designed for the purpose intended. For example, the use of prenumbered shipping documents is an essential element to the controls that ensure that all goods shipped have been billed. Similarly, the use of prenumbered sales invoices is desirable to make sure that billings have been recorded. The special characteristics of properly designed documents and records were discussed in Chapter 1.

Authorization of transactions. There are five authorizations for sales and cash receipts transactions, each of which should be indicated by initialing the appropriate document:

1. Approval of credit before shipment takes place.

2. Shipment of the goods.

3. Determination of appropriate price to charge for the goods. Price includes terms and freight.

4. Approval of credits to accounts receivable for such things as sales returns and allowances or write-off of uncollectible accounts.

5. Determining cash discounts allowed for customers' payments made before the discount date.

Separation of the custody of assets from accounting. The person responsible for shipping goods or receiving cash should have no accounting responsibility. Without adequate segregation of duties, the potential for fraud increases.

Independent checks on performance. There are several appropriate types of internal verification, including:

- Account for all prenumbered shipping documents. This control helps ensure that all shipments have been billed.

- Account for all prenumbered sales invoices. This control helps to ensure that all sales invoices have been recorded.

- Compare prices on invoices charged to customers for shipments to a price list approved by management.

- Check the footing in journals and records.

- Reconcile the accounts receivable control account to the related subsidiary ledger.

- Prepare a monthly bank reconciliation. One of the most important controls used by accountants is a bank reconciliation. This control is discussed in greater detail in Chapter 4.

Monthly statements to customers. Monthly statements to customers provide a check on the accuracy of both the seller's and buyer's records.

SUMMARY

Chapter 3 is a study of:

- The nature of the transactions in the sales and cash receipts cycle.

- The documents and records used to record and summarize transactions in the cycle.

- A method of recording sales and cash receipts transactions.

- Common internal controls for the cycle.

To better understand the chapter material, a comprehensive example of the relationships among the different parts of the cycle is provided in Figure 3-9 (pages 48 and 49). Five simple transactions are used to illustrate the most common documents and records in the system and the way the documents are used to record transactions.

A suggested method of studying the material in Figure 3-9 is to trace each transaction from its source to its final recording in the general ledger. Special emphasis should be put on examining the source of the accounts receivable trial balance and its relationship to the subsidiary ledger and control account.

After the documents, records, and recording methods in Figure 3-9 are understood, the totals in each general ledger account should be traced to the year-end worksheet in Figure 1-8 on page 18.

Notice that the shaded portion of each general ledger account shows the adjusting entries. The balance above the shaded area will therefore be in the unadjusted trial balance columns and the final ledger balance will be in the adjusted trial balance columns in Figure 1-8.

FIGURE 3-9
Illustrative Sales and Cash Receipts Cycle
Transactions Using Documents and Records
Commonly Found in the Cycle

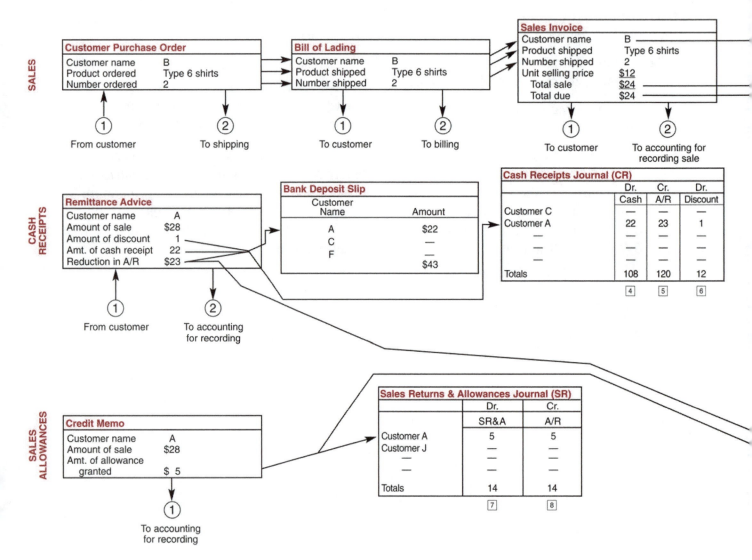

SALES

Customer Purchase Order

Customer name	B
Product ordered	Type 6 shirts
Number ordered	2

① From customer

② To shipping

Bill of Lading

Customer name	B
Product shipped	Type 6 shirts
Number shipped	2

① To customer

② To billing

Sales Invoice

Customer name	B
Product shipped	Type 6 shirts
Number shipped	2
Unit selling price	$12
Total sale	$24
Total due	$24

① To customer

② To accounting for recording sale

CASH RECEIPTS

Remittance Advice

Customer name	A
Amount of sale	$28
Amount of discount	1
Amt. of cash receipt	22
Reduction in A/R	$23

① From customer

② To accounting for recording

Bank Deposit Slip

Customer Name	Amount
A	$22
C	—
F	—
	$43

Cash Receipts Journal (CR)

	Dr. Cash	Cr. A/R	Dr. Discount
Customer C	—	—	—
Customer A	22	23	1
	—	—	—
	—	—	—
	—	—	—
Totals	108	120	12
	☐4	☐5	☐6

SALES ALLOWANCES

Credit Memo

Customer name	A
Amount of sale	$28
Amt. of allowance granted	$ 5

① To accounting for recording

Sales Returns & Allowances Journal (SR)

	Dr. SR&A	Cr. A/R
Customer A	5	5
Customer J	—	—
	—	—
	—	—
Totals	14	14
	☐7	☐8

BAD DEBT EXPENSE

INFORMATION ABOUT BAD DEBT EXPENSE:

Percent of net sales on account	2%
Net sales on account	$2,467
Bad debt expense estimate	$ 49

WRITE-OFF OF ACCT. REC.

INFORMATION ABOUT UNCOLLECTIBLE A/R:

Customer F	$ 26

General Journal (GJ)

	Dr.	Cr.
Bad Debt Expense	49		☐9
Allowance for Doubtful Accts.		49	☐10
Allowance for Doubtful Accts.	26		☐11
Accts. Receivable		26	☐12

48

Five transactions — December 2013

1. Sale — 2 type 6 shirts at $12 each — customer B
2. Collection — $22 on outstanding accounts receivable — customer A — sales discount $1
3. Sales allowance — $5 allowance on outstanding accounts receivable — customer A
4. Bad debt expense — yearly provision at 2% of annual net sales on account
5. Write-off of account receivable — it was determined that amount due from customer F would not be collected

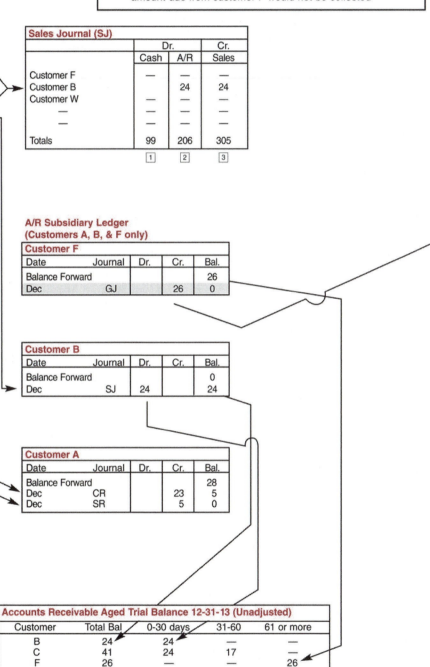

Sales Journal (SJ)

	Dr.		Cr.
	Cash	A/R	Sales
Customer F	—		
Customer B		24	24
Customer W	—	—	—
	—	—	—
	—	—	—
Totals	99	206	305
	☐1	☐2	☐3

**A/R Subsidiary Ledger
(Customers A, B, & F only)**

Customer F

Date	Journal	Dr.	Cr.	Bal.
Balance Forward				26
Dec	GJ		26	0

Customer B

Date	Journal	Dr.	Cr.	Bal.
Balance Forward				0
Dec	SJ	24		24

Customer A

Date	Journal	Dr.	Cr.	Bal.
Balance Forward				28
Dec	CR		23	5
Dec	SR		5	0

Accounts Receivable Aged Trial Balance 12-31-13 (Unadjusted)

Customer	Total Bal	0-30 days	31-60	61 or more
B	24	24	—	—
C	41	24	17	—
F	26	—	—	26
}	}	}	}	}
Total	298	226	37	35

△

GENERAL LEDGER ACCOUNTS

Cash in Bank

Mo.	Jr.	Dr.	Cr.	Bal.
Balance Forward				91
☐1 Dec	SJ	99		
☐4 Dec	CR	108		298 *
—	—	—	—	—

Accounts Receivable

Mo.	Jr.	Dr.	Cr.	Bal.
Balance Forward				226
☐2 Dec	SJ	206		
☐5 Dec	CR		120	
☐8 Dec	SR		14	298 △
☐12 Dec	GJ		26	272

Sales

Mo.	Jr.	Dr.	Cr.	Bal.
Balance Forward				3343
☐3 Dec	SJ		305	3648

Sales Discounts Taken

Mo.	Jr.	Dr.	Cr.	Bal.
Balance Forward				170
☐6 Dec	CR	12		182

Sales Returns & Allowances

Mo.	Jr.	Dr.	Cr.	Bal.
Balance Forward				200
☐7 Dec	SR	14		214

Bad Debt Expense

Mo.	Jr.	Dr.	Cr.	Bal.
Balance Forward				0
☐9 Dec	GJ	49		49

Allowance for Doubtful Accounts

Mo.	Jr.	Dr.	Cr.	Bal.
Balance Forward				18
☐10 Dec	GJ		49	67
☐11 Dec	GJ	26		41

☐ — posted to general ledger

△ — trial balance reconciles to control account

***This balance will not tie to the unadjusted trial balance
(Fig. 1-8) because cash disbursements have not yet been posted.**

This page is intentionally blank.

CHAPTER 4

Purchases and Cash Disbursements Cycle

This chapter discusses the transactions, documents, and records in the purchases and cash disbursements cycle. First, an overview is provided for each of the four subcycles of the overall cycle. The remainder of the chapter covers the actions in each subcycle and the transactions resulting from those actions.

The purchases and cash disbursements cycle starts with the preparation of a written or oral purchase requisition for goods or services and ends with the disbursement of cash to pay for the purchase and the recording of the disbursement.

The most important difference between the purchases and cash disbursements cycle and the sales and cash receipts cycle is the large number of account balances affected in the purchases and cash disbursements cycle. The table below lists a few account balances affected by purchases and cash disbursements.

The similarities between the two cycles are far greater than the differences. The sales of one company are the purchases of another. Similarly, the cash disbursements of one company become the cash receipts of another. A complete understanding of sales and cash receipts helps one understand purchases and cash disbursements.

Asset Accounts	Liability Accounts	Expense Accounts
Cash in bank	Accounts payable	Interest
Fixed assets	Accrued expenses	Repair and maintenance
Inventory	Payroll taxes payable	Utilities
Prepaid expenses	Notes payable	Property taxes
Marketable securities	Mortgages payable	Depreciation

SUBCYCLES, ACTIONS, COMMON TRANSACTIONS, AND TYPICAL ACCOUNTS AFFECTED

There are four primary subcycles in the purchases and cash disbursements cycle. Several actions take place in each subcycle. The recording of these actions results in transactions, which in turn result in changes in account balances. The four subcycles are shown on the following page.

Subcycles	Actions	Common Transactions	Typical Account Balances Affected
Purchases	Process purchase orders, receive goods, record purchase in journal and subsidiary ledger, summarize journal and post to general ledger.	Cash purchases Credit purchases	Inventory Cash Accounts payable Fixed assets Repair and maintenance
Cash disbursements	Disburse cash, record cash disbursements in journal and subsidiary ledger, summarize journal and post to general ledger.	Payments on accounts payable Payments on notes	Cash Accounts payable Purchases discounts Notes payable
Purchases returns and allowances	Request purchase return or allowance, return goods, record in journal and subsidiary ledger, summarize journal and post to general ledger.	Purchases returns Purchases allowances	Accounts payable Purchases returns and allowances
Provision for depreciation, and adjustments for prepaids and accruals	Determine appropriate adjustments, record in general journal and post to general ledger.	Depreciation Income tax provision Interest expense provision	Depreciation expense Income tax expense Income taxes payable Interest payable

ACCOUNTANT'S OBJECTIVES

The accountant's objectives in recording transactions in the purchases and cash disbursements cycle and summarizing the resultant account balances are essentially the same as for sales and cash receipts. They are as follows:

1. All existing transactions for each subcycle are recorded.

2. All transactions are recorded and summarized at the correct amounts.

3. All transactions are correctly classified as defined by the chart of accounts.

4. All transactions are included in the proper period.

5. All material disclosures affecting the accounts are included in the financial statements and related footnotes.

PURCHASES — ACTIONS AND RELATED DOCUMENTS

Figure 4-1 (page 53) includes a flowchart of the actions and related documents for purchases in a typical company. A discussion of the information in the flowchart follows.

FIGURE 4-1
Purchases — Actions and Related Documents

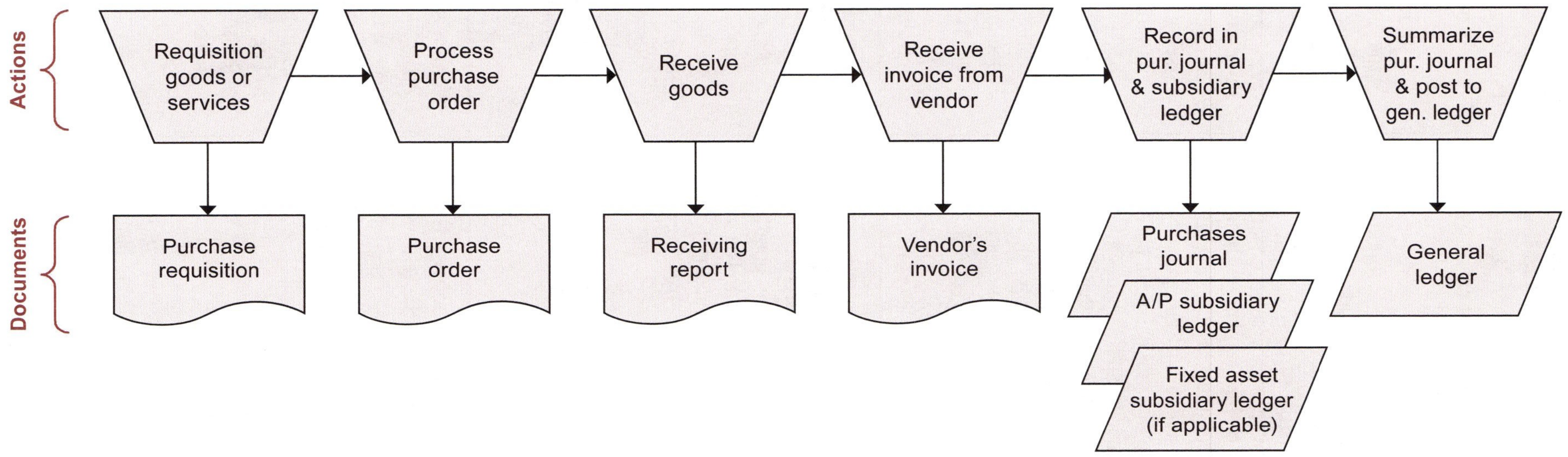

Actions

| Requisition goods or services | Process purchase order | Receive goods | Receive invoice from vendor | Record in pur. journal & subsidiary ledger | Summarize pur. journal & post to gen. ledger |

Documents

| Purchase requisition | Purchase order | Receiving report | Vendor's invoice | Purchases journal / A/P subsidiary ledger / Fixed asset subsidiary ledger (if applicable) | General ledger |

ACTIONS	DOCUMENTS
Requisition goods or services — A written or oral request for goods or services by the client's personnel is the starting point for the system. It may take the form of a request for such purchases as materials by a foreman or the storeroom supervisor, outside repairs by office or factory personnel, or insurance by the vice president in charge of fixed assets.	**Purchase requisition** — A document prepared to inform the purchasing department of goods or services needed by other units in a company. It indicates the goods or services requested, the quantity desired, and the date needed. Many times the request is oral, but a written requisition form is preferred.
Process purchase order — The purchasing department receives the purchase requisition and initiates the order for the goods. The primary function of the purchasing department is to order only goods and services that are needed and to order from vendors that can supply, on a timely basis, the appropriate quantity of a good or service that is of satisfactory quality at the desired price.	**Purchase order** — A document prepared requesting goods or services from a vendor (seller). The purchase order should include the name and address of the vendor, the goods or services desired, and the desired delivery or performance date. The order is usually in writing and is a legal document that is an offer to buy. When it is received by the vendor, the document is referred to as a customer purchase order. Thus the same document is called a purchase order by the buyer and a customer purchase order by the seller.
Receive goods or services — In most cases, generally accepted accounting principles require the recognition of a purchase transaction as of the date when the goods are received or services are performed. The actual receipt of goods or services and the related documentation of the receipt are therefore essential to proper recording of a purchase transaction.	**Receiving report** — A document prepared at the time tangible goods are received. The report indicates the description and condition of the goods, the quantity received, and the date received. The same information should be included on the buyer's receiving report as on the seller's shipping document. If the same quantity of goods was received as was ordered, the information on the purchase order and the receiving report should be the same. Frequently companies use an extra copy of the purchase order as a receiving report rather than prepare a different form.
Receive invoice from vendor — Shortly after the goods or services are received, the seller sends a bill. Most companies record transactions on the basis of the vendor's invoice because it includes unit cost, transportation, and the total amount due. As a practical matter, many companies also record the liability for goods or services on the date the invoice is received. If a company follows this procedure, great care must be taken to establish proper accounts payable cutoff at year-end. A liability must be recorded for all goods and services received prior to year-end, regardless of the dates invoices are received.	**Vendor's invoice** — A document received from the vendor indicating the description and quantity of goods or services received, the price including freight, the cash discount terms, and the date of the billing. It specifies the amount of money owed to the vendor for a purchase. The document is called a "sales invoice" by the seller. The buyer and seller simply call the same form different names.

ACTIONS	DOCUMENTS
Record in purchases journal and subsidiary ledger — The purchases journal is the record of original entry for purchase transactions. As for sales, every purchase transaction must be recorded in the purchases journal, individually or in summary form. Every purchase on account should also be recorded in the accounts payable subsidiary ledger as an increase in payables. A purchase might also affect the fixed asset or marketable securities subsidiary ledger.	**Purchases journal** — A journal for recording purchases of goods and services. It is essentially the same as a sales journal except for the nature of the transactions. The purchases journal usually includes more columns than a sales journal because of the larger number of accounts involved. It usually includes several classifications for the most significant types of purchases, such as the purchase of inventory, repairs and maintenance, and supplies. There is also a column for miscellaneous debits and credits and a column for the credit to accounts payable.

Accounts payable subsidiary ledger — A ledger for recording individual purchases, cash disbursements, and purchases returns and allowances for each vendor. The accounts payable subsidiary ledger performs the same function as the accounts receivable subsidiary ledger. The total of the individual account balances in the subsidiary ledger equals the total balance of accounts payable in the general ledger.

Fixed asset subsidiary ledger — A ledger for recording individual purchases of fixed assets. Frequently a separate subsidiary exists for each classification of fixed assets, such as delivery equipment or office furniture.

A unique characteristic of the typical fixed asset subsidiary ledger is the existence of three subsidiaries in one: gross fixed assets, depreciation expense, and accumulated depreciation. A subsidiary ledger for fixed assets ordinarily includes original cost, current depreciation on the asset, and accumulated depreciation to date. The total cost of the assets in a given classification of fixed assets equals the balance in the general ledger for that classification. Similarly, the depreciation and accumulated depreciation totals also equal the respective general ledger balances. |
| **Summarize purchases journal and post to general ledger** – As with sales, the purchases journal is totaled periodically, usually monthly. The totals are posted to the general ledger. | **General ledger** — A record used to summarize transactions recorded in the journals. Only the totals in the purchases journal are posted to the general ledger. For the miscellaneous debit and credit columns in the purchases journal, the total for each account affected must be posted to the general ledger.

(continued on following page) |

ACTIONS	DOCUMENTS
	For example, assume the miscellaneous debit column totaled $30 and included four transactions.

Trans. #	Acct. #	Dr. Amt.
1	309	$ 6
2	614	14
3	309	7
4	614	3
		$ 30

The totals posted to the general ledger are $13 for account #309 and $17 for account #614.

CASH DISBURSEMENTS — ACTIONS AND RELATED DOCUMENTS

There are usually two types of disbursements: (1) payments on accounts payable or payments on other liabilities such as notes or mortgages and (2) purchases for cash. Cash purchases include cash paid on delivery for purchases of goods and services and petty cash transactions.

Most companies record all cash disbursements by check in the cash disbursements journal. Therefore, some purchases of goods and services are first recorded only in the cash disbursements journal and not in the purchases journal.

The cash disbursements cycle is similar to the one discussed for cash receipts. The major differences are:

- A check is prepared and sent for disbursements rather than cash being received.

- Checks are prenumbered and therefore easier to control than cash receipts.

Figure 4-2 includes a flowchart of the actions and related documents for cash disbursements in a typical company. A discussion of the information in the flowchart follows.

FIGURE 4-2
Cash Disbursements — Actions and Related Documents

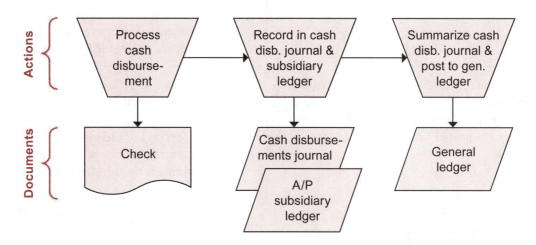

ACTIONS	DOCUMENTS
Process cash disbursement — The preparation, signing, and mailing of a check are essential actions in the cash disbursements subcycle. The delivery or mailing date of the check is the cash disbursement cutoff date according to generally accepted accounting principles. The check is prepared from the information on the vendor's invoice, receiving report, and purchase order. When these documents do not exist, such as for the payment of rent, other documents or records are used to indicate when payment is due.	**Check** — A document prepared to pay for a purchase when payment is due. After the check is signed by an authorized person, it is an asset. When cashed by the vendor and cleared by the client's bank, it is referred to as a cancelled check. The check must include the payee, amount, and date. Some companies prepare one or more copies for record keeping.
Record in cash disbursements journal and subsidiary ledger — The cash disbursements journal is the record of original entry for cash disbursement transactions. This journal should look almost the same as the purchases, sales, and cash receipts journals except for differences in the account titles. The only subsidiary ledger usually affected by cash disbursements is accounts payable. The accounts payable subsidiary ledger is the same ledger described earlier as a part of purchases.	**Cash disbursements journal** — A journal for recording cash disbursements. It indicates total cash paid, the debit to accounts payable at the gross amount of the original purchase, cash discounts taken, and other debits and credits. The daily entries in the cash disbursements journal are supported by copies of checks or other documents such as vendors' invoices. In the same manner as for accounts receivable, the accountant must use care in recording the debit to accounts payable in the cash disbursements journal so that it is consistent with the recording of the original purchase. When an account payable is fully paid, the accounts payable subsidiary ledger must reflect a zero balance. **Accounts payable subsidiary ledger** — See Purchases (page 55).
Summarize cash disbursements journal and post to general ledger — The concepts are the same for this action as for purchases and are not repeated.	**General ledger** — See Purchases (page 55).

PURCHASES RETURNS AND ALLOWANCES — ACTIONS AND RELATED DOCUMENTS

A purchase return is the return of merchandise to the vendor for such reasons as the incorrect product being sent or defective merchandise. The buyer keeps the goods when there is a purchase allowance but is granted a reduced purchase price.

The actions and recording of purchases returns and allowances are almost identical to those for sales returns and allowances; however, instead of a decrease in accounts receivable there is a decrease in accounts payable.

Figure 4-3 shows the actions and related documents, which are then discussed in more detail.

FIGURE 4-3
Purchases Returns and Allowances — Actions and Related Documents

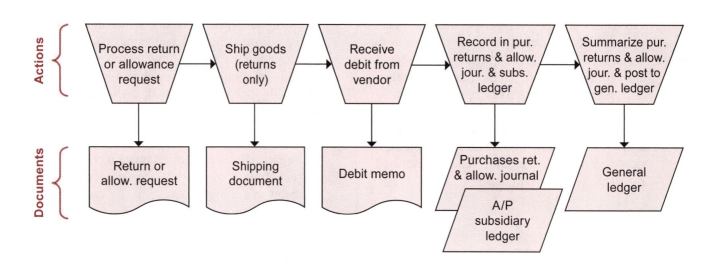

ACTIONS	DOCUMENTS
Process return or allowance request — A request for authority to return goods or be granted a reduction in purchase price is the starting point for recording the return of goods or an allowance. Typically, these are originated by the purchasing department. It is common for the parties to negotiate the amount of the credit.	**Return or allowance request** — A document prepared to request authority to return goods or obtain an allowance. The form must state whether the transaction is a return or an allowance, and the amount of the credit granted. The form is the same one described for sales returns and allowances. The perspective is now that of the purchaser requesting the return or allowance rather than the seller authorizing the return or allowance.

ACTIONS	DOCUMENTS
Ship goods (returns only) — Contrary to sales returns and allowances, the procedures for generally accepted accounting principles require the recognition of purchase returns and allowances in the accounting period of the return of the goods. For most companies, purchase returns and allowances are not material.	**Shipping document** — A document prepared at the time the goods are returned to the vendor. This document is often the same type used for shipments of goods to customers. When that is the case, it must be clearly indicated on the document that it is a purchase return and not a sale.
Receive debit from vendor — The debit from the vendor performs the same function as the vendor's invoice—they both inform customers of a change in accounts payable. The vendor's invoice informs the customer of an increase and the debit a decrease.	**Debit memo** — A document received from the vendor indicating the amount and terms of the return or allowance. It is much like a vendor's invoice, but it reduces the amount owed to the vendor.
Record in purchases returns and allowances journal and subsidiary ledger — The purchases returns and allowances journal is the record of original entry for purchases returns and allowances. Like the sales returns and allowances journal, it can be a separate journal or a part of the purchases journal.	**Purchases returns and allowances journal** — A journal for recording purchases returns and allowances. It is common to record purchases returns and allowances in the purchases journal, using a separate column. **Accounts payable subsidiary ledger** — See Purchases (page 55).
Summarize purchases returns and allowances journal and post to general ledger — The concepts for this action are the same as for purchases and cash disbursements, and are not repeated.	**General ledger** — See Purchases (page 55).

PREPAIDS, ACCRUALS, AND DEPRECIATION — ACTIONS AND RELATED DOCUMENTS

Prepaids, accruals, and depreciation are adjustments to the financial statements to reflect the accrual method of accounting. Common examples of adjustments to prepaids are for prepaid insurance or rent. Typical accruals are for unpaid interest and property taxes. Depreciation is the periodic amortization of the purchase of fixed assets. The concepts and related documents for prepaids, accruals and depreciation are essentially the same as for bad debt expense, which was discussed in Chapter 3.

The actions and related documents for accruals, prepaids, and depreciation are shown in Figure 4-4 (page 60). A discussion of the information in the flowchart follows.

To illustrate the actions and related documents for accruals, prepaids, and depreciation, an accrual for unpaid interest is shown. The same concepts are followed for other accruals, prepaids, and depreciation.

FIGURE 4-4
Prepaids, Accruals, and Depreciation — Actions and Related Documents

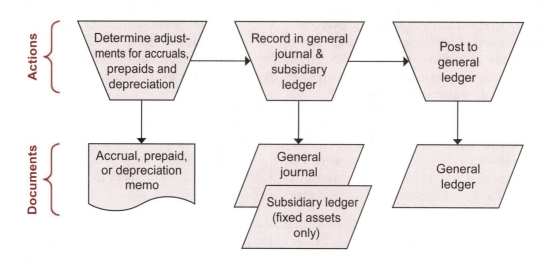

ACTIONS	DOCUMENTS
Determine accrual for unpaid interest — When financial statements are prepared, the amount of the accrual is calculated at the balance sheet date. For example, assume the balance sheet date of a company is April 30 and the company has one note payable for $10,000 bearing interest at 12% annually. The note is dated April 1 and has not had an interest payment to date. The accrued interest should be $100 ($10,000 x 12% x 1/12). If the balance in the general ledger for accrued interest before the adjustment is $30, the adjustment is a debit to interest expense and a credit to accrued interest of $70.	**Accrued interest memo** — A document indicating the accrual for interest at the balance sheet date. Many companies do not prepare this document. Instead, a separate file can be maintained showing the basis on which the periodic accrual is made.
Record in general journal — The general journal is the journal of original entry for accrued interest and the related expense. The entry is usually recorded as a debit to interest expense and a credit to accrued interest. If the balance in the accrual account before the adjustment is larger than the ending balance is supposed to be, the debit is to accrued interest and the credit is to interest expense.	**General journal** — A journal for recording transactions not recorded in specialized journals. Transactions such as accruals for unpaid interest, where there is only one transaction for each month, are recorded in the general journal. The journal has two columns, one for debits and a second for credits. **Subsidiary ledger** — Not applicable for accrued interest.
Post to general ledger — See bad debt expense in Chapter 3 (page 43).	**General ledger** — See Sales (page 37).

ACCOUNTS PAYABLE TRIAL BALANCE

The accounts payable trial balance is a listing of the ending balances in the accounts payable subsidiary ledger at a specific point in time. It includes only a column for individual unpaid account balances. In contrast to accounts receivable, an aged analysis of accounts payable is ordinarily not prepared because companies are less concerned about unpaid payables than uncollected receivables. An illustration of a typical accounts payable trial balance is shown in Figure 4-5.

FIGURE 4-5
Accounts Payable Trial Balance

Anycompany, Inc.
Accounts Payable Trial Balance
December 31, 2013

VENDOR NO.	VENDOR NAME	AMOUNT PAYABLE
2819	Smith Brothers Sports Equipment	$ 334.55
1237	Jumpin' Jack's, Inc.	127.49
4598	Chicago Sports Authority	537.95
	TOTAL	$ 999.99

FIXED ASSETS TRIAL BALANCE

The fixed assets trial balance is a listing of the ending balances in the fixed assets subsidiary ledger at a specific point in time, usually accounting year-end, for both original cost and accumulated depreciation. The trial balance also typically includes the net book value. Obviously, for the net book value to be accurate, depreciation must be calculated and recorded through the date of the trial balance. A separate trial balance is prepared for each fixed assets general ledger account if there is more than one. An illustration of a typical fixed assets trial balance is shown in Figure 4-6.

FIGURE 4-6
Fixed Assets Trial Balance

Anycompany, Inc.
Fixed Assets Trial Balance
December 31, 2013

ASSET	COST	ACCUM. DEPREC.	NET BOOK VALUE
Furniture	$ 6,456.78	$ 2,400.00	$ 4,056.78
Truck	22,378.22	12,676.40	9,701.82
Copier	1,875.00	823.60	1,051.40
Computer	14,290.00	4,100.00	10,190.00
TOTALS	$45,000.00	$20,000.00	$25,000.00

INTERNAL CONTROLS

The most important internal controls for purchases and cash disbursements are as follows:

Adequate documents and records. The documents described for purchases, purchases returns and allowances, and cash disbursements should be pre-numbered and designed for the purpose intended. For example, the use of prenumbered receiving reports is essential to help a company be sure that all merchandise receipts have been recorded. The special characteristics of properly designed documents and records were discussed in Chapter 1.

Authorization of transactions. There are four key authorizations for purchases and cash disbursements, each of which should be indicated by initialing the appropriate document.

1. Authorization to order goods or services, including quantity — A person at the appropriate level should approve all purchases to prevent overbuying or buying goods or services that are not needed.

2. Authorization of price — To assure buying goods at the lowest cost, given the quality and service needs of the buyer. Many companies use a purchasing department.

3. Authorization to receive the goods or services — When the goods or services are delivered, approval is needed to be sure the appropriate items have been received.

4. Authorization to disburse cash — The signing of a check by an authorized person is the approval for payment. That person should examine supporting documentation to make sure that payment is appropriate.

Separation of the custody of assets from accounting. The person responsible for receiving goods or signing checks should have no accounting responsibility. Without adequate segregation of duties, the potential for fraud increases.

Independent checks on performance. There are several appropriate types of independent checks, including:

- Account for all receiving reports. This control helps ensure that all accounts payable have been recorded.

- Check prices actually paid for goods against those available from local stores, catalogs, and price lists. The purpose is to determine that prices paid for goods and services are reasonable.

- Check the mathematical accuracy of journals and records.

- Reconcile all control accounts to the related subsidiary ledgers. Examples include accounts payable and fixed assets.

- Prepare a monthly bank reconciliation. One of the most important controls used by companies is a bank reconciliation. When performed by a person independent of those who handle the cash or are responsible for accounting records involving cash, the bank reconciliation is useful in uncovering both unintentional errors and fraud. This control is of sufficient importance to merit study in more detail.

BANK RECONCILIATION

A bank reconciliation is the determination of the reasons for the differences (reconciling items) between the cash in the bank balance as stated on the bank statement and on the general ledger at a point in time. Common causes of the differences include:

- Deposits recorded in the books in one period but not deposited until the next period (deposits in transit).

- Checks recorded and mailed in one period but not clearing the bank until the next period (outstanding checks).

- Bank service charges not recorded in the books until the period following the bank's deduction of them from the bank balance.

A bank reconciliation can also be used to locate errors or fraud in the accounting records and bank errors. There are several types of errors or fraud that a carefully prepared bank reconciliation should uncover. Examples include:

- A check recorded at a different amount from the actual amount of the check.

- A deposit to the bank that the bookkeeper forgot to record in the cash receipts journal.

- The theft of cash by not depositing money. The bank reconciliation will uncover this only if the receipt of cash was recorded in the cash receipts journal.

- The bank debiting a customer's account for a larger amount than the amount of the check (bank error).
- An error in adding the cash receipts column in the cash receipts journal.
- Posting the wrong total of the cash disbursements column in the cash disbursements journal to the general ledger.

Preparation of a bank reconciliation. A bank reconciliation should be prepared only after all accounting transactions for the month have been recorded and posted to the general ledger, and the bank statement has been received from the bank. An example of a bank reconciliation for Jones Co. is included in Figure 4-7.

The form of the bank reconciliation in Figure 4-7 shows a distinction between two types of reconciling items: timing differences and items requiring adjustment of the general ledger balance.

Timing differences result from the bank and company processing transactions at a different time. There are three common types of timing differences: deposits in transit, outstanding checks and errors by the bank that they will correct. Only timing differences are included in the left column of the bank reconciliation. In Figure 4-7 there are two types of timing differences: deposits in transit and outstanding checks.

FIGURE 4-7
Bank Reconciliation and Related Adjusting Journal Entries

Bank Reconciliation — Jones Co.
November 30, 2013

	Bank Statement	General Ledger
Unadjusted balance 11-30-13	$ 326.10	$ 378.00
Add: Deposits in transit		

	Amount		
11-29-13	$ 75.00		
11-30-13	25.00		
Total		100.00	

Deduct: Outstanding checks

Check #	Amount		
267	$ 6.37		
281	21.14		
282	8.59		
Total		(36.10)	

	Bank Statement	General Ledger
Adjustments:		
Recording error (Ck. #306)		20.00
Bank service charge		(8.00)
Adjusted balance 11-30-13	$390.00	$390.00

Adjusting Journal Entries
November 2013

	DR.	CR.
1. Cash in bank	20.00	
Accounts payable		20.00

Error in recording check #306. $57.25 recorded in CD journal less $37.25 check amount = $20.00 error.

	DR.	CR.
2. Bank service charges	8.00	
Cash in bank		8.00

To record November bank service charges.

Items requiring adjustment of the general ledger are receipts and disbursements processed by the bank, but not yet recorded, and errors by the company. Bank service charges, unrecorded checks, and checks recorded at the wrong amounts are examples. Only items requiring adjustment are included in the right column of the bank reconciliation.

An adjusting entry is also required for each error adjustment included in the general ledger column. The bank reconciliation in Figure 4-7 includes one adjustment for a recording error and one for an unrecorded bank service charge.

To prepare a bank reconciliation, the following documents and records for a given period are required.

- Bank statement, including all cancelled checks and deposit slips for the period or a list of cancelled checks and deposits.

- Cash receipts journal.

- Cash disbursements journal.

- Cash-in-bank general ledger account.

- Prior month's bank reconciliation.

A description of the reconciliation procedure follows with references to the bank reconciliation in Figure 4-7 in parenthesis:

1. Begin the reconciliation by writing in the ending balance on the bank statement and the general ledger balance for cash on the bank reconciliation ($326.10 and $378.00).

2. Trace all cash receipts transactions from (a) deposits in transit in the prior month's bank reconciliation and (b) the current period cash receipts journal to the current period bank statement.

   Any amounts that have not been deposited are deposits in transit. They are listed on the bank reconciliation (two totaling $100.00).

Deposits included in the bank statement but not recorded or differences between the amount of recorded cash receipts and the recorded deposits must be investigated. Either the bank is in error or an adjustment is required to the company's records.

3. Trace all cash disbursement transactions from the list of (a) outstanding checks on the prior month's bank reconciliation and (b) the current period cash disbursements journal to the list of checks or actual checks clearing the bank. For each transaction, compare the check number, payee, and amount.

   All cancelled checks included with the bank statement must be matched with their recorded entries in the cash disbursements journal. Prior month's outstanding checks and other recorded checks that have not cleared are outstanding checks and must be listed on the bank reconciliation (three totaling $36.10).

   Checks clearing the bank that have not been recorded or checks clearing the bank for a different amount must be investigated. Either the bank is in error or an adjustment is required to the company's records ($20.00 error).

4. Account for all items in the beginning-of-the-period bank reconciliation, cash receipts and disbursements journals, and bank statement that have not already been accounted for in steps 2 and 3. Common examples of additional reconciling items on the bank statement are bank service charges and collections by the bank of notes receivable credited directly to the bank account. These items will require adjusting entries ($8.00 adjustment for bank service charge).

5. Make the adjusting journal entries for the adjustments to the general ledger balance (two adjusting entries).

6. Foot the bank reconciliation and compare the adjusted bank balance to the general ledger after the adjustments have been made. If the balances do not agree, there is an error in preparing the bank reconciliation, a math error in totaling the journals or general ledger, a bank error, or possibly even a theft of cash. (In Figure 4-7, both totals foot to $390.00.)

SUMMARY

Chapter 4 is a study of:

- The nature of the transactions in the purchases and cash disbursements cycle.

- The documents and records used to record and summarize transactions in the cycle.

- A method of recording purchases and cash disbursements transactions.

- Common internal controls for the cycle.

- Bank reconciliations.

To better understand the chapter material, a comprehensive example of the relationships among the different parts of the cycle is provided in Figure 4-8 (pages 66 and 67). Four simple transactions are used to illustrate the most common documents and records in the cycle, and the way the documents are used to record transactions.

A suggested method of studying the material in Figure 4-8 is to trace each transaction from its source to its final recording in the general ledger. Special emphasis should be placed on examining the source of the accounts payable trial balance and its relationship to the subsidiary ledger and control account.

After the documents, records, and recording methods in Figure 4-8 are understood, the totals in each general ledger account should be traced to the year-end worksheet in Figure 1-8 on page 18. Notice that the shaded portion of each general ledger account shows the adjusting entries. The balance above the shaded area will therefore be in the unadjusted trial balance columns and the final ledger balance will be in the adjusted trial balance columns in Figure 1-8.

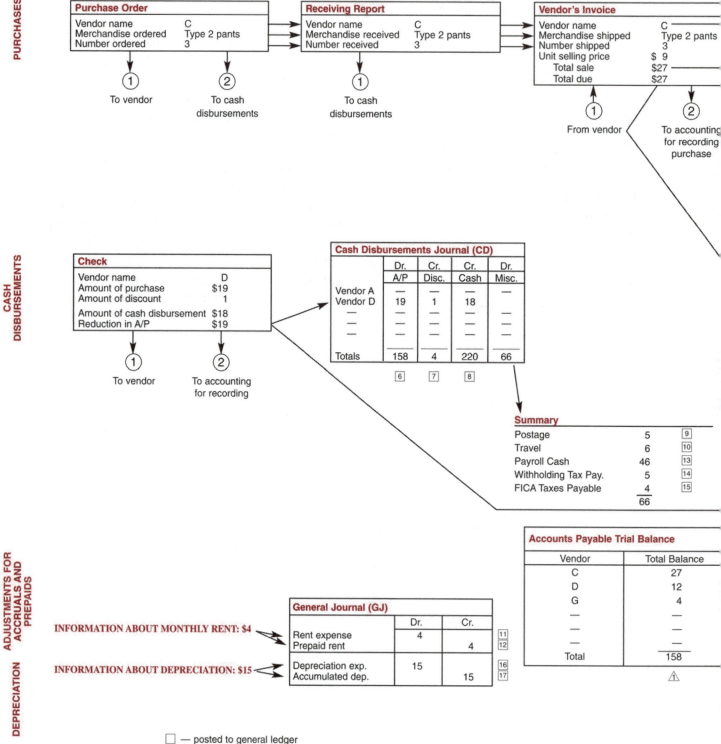

FIGURE 4-8
Illustrative Purchases and Cash Disbursements Cycle Transactions Using Documents and Records Commonly Found in the Cycle

PURCHASES

Purchase Order

Vendor name	C
Merchandise ordered	Type 2 pants
Number ordered	3

① To vendor ② To cash disbursements

Receiving Report

Vendor name	C
Merchandise received	Type 2 pants
Number received	3

① To cash disbursements

Vendor's Invoice

Vendor name	C
Merchandise shipped	Type 2 pants
Number shipped	3
Unit selling price	$ 9
Total sale	$27
Total due	$27

① From vendor ② To accounting for recording purchase

CASH DISBURSEMENTS

Check

Vendor name	D
Amount of purchase	$19
Amount of discount	1
Amount of cash disbursement	$18
Reduction in A/P	$19

① To vendor ② To accounting for recording

Cash Disbursements Journal (CD)

	Dr. A/P	Cr. Disc.	Cr. Cash	Dr. Misc.
Vendor A	—	—	—	—
Vendor D	19	1	18	—
	—	—	—	—
	—	—	—	—
	—	—	—	—
	—	—	—	—
Totals	158	4	220	66

6   7   8

Summary

Postage	5	9
Travel	6	10
Payroll Cash	46	13
Withholding Tax Pay.	5	14
FICA Taxes Payable	4	15
	66	

ADJUSTMENTS FOR ACCRUALS AND PREPAIDS

INFORMATION ABOUT MONTHLY RENT: $4

DEPRECIATION

INFORMATION ABOUT DEPRECIATION: $15

General Journal (GJ)

	Dr.	Cr.
Rent expense	4	
Prepaid rent		4
Depreciation exp.	15	
Accumulated dep.		15

11 12 16 17

Accounts Payable Trial Balance

Vendor	Total Balance
C	27
D	12
G	4
—	—
—	—
—	—
Total	158

△

☐ — posted to general ledger
△ — trial balance reconciles to control account
*☐ — posted to general ledger from payroll
journal (PR) and general journal (GJ) — see Figure 5-3

Four Transactions — December 2013

1. Purchase — 3 type 2 pants at $9 each — Vendor C (purchase requisition not included)
2. Cash disbursement — $19 on outstanding accounts payable — Vendor D — purchase discount $1
3. Prepaid rent expense — adjustment for one month's rent of $4
4. One year's depreciation on delivery equipment — $15

Purchases Journal (PJ)

	Dr.		Cr.
	Purchases	Misc. Dr.	A/P
Vendor A	—	—	—
Vendor C	27	—	27
Vendor X	—	—	—
—	—	—	—
—	—	—	—
Totals	183	27	210
	[1]		[2]

Summary

Prepaid rent	8	[3]
Repair expense	13	[4]
Utility expense	6	[5]
	27	

A/P Subsidiary Ledger
(Vendors C, D, and G only)

Vendor C

Date	Journal	Dr.	Cr.	Bal.
Balance Forward				0
Dec	(PJ)		27	27

Vendor D

Date	Journal	Dr.	Cr.	Bal.
Balance Forward				31
Dec	CD	19		12

Vendor G

Date	Journal	Dr.	Cr.	Bal.
Balance Forward				4

Payroll Cash (Imprest)

Mo.	Jr.	Dr.	Cr.	Bal.
Balance Forward				5
*[5] Dec	PR		46	
[13] Dec	CD	46		5

Withholding Taxes Payable

Mo.	Jr.	Dr.	Cr.	Bal.
Balance Forward				5
*[3] Dec	PR		6	
[14] Dec	CD	5		6

FICA Taxes Payable

Mo.	Jr.	Dr.	Cr.	Bal.
Balance Forward				4
*[4] Dec	PR		5	
[15] Dec	CD	4		5
*[10] Dec	GJ		5	10

GENERAL LEDGER ACCOUNTS

Cash in Bank

Mo.	Jr.	Dr.	Cr.	Bal.
Balance Forward				91
Dec	SJ	99		
Dec	CR	108		
[8] Dec	CD		220	78

Accounts Payable

Mo.	Jr.	Dr.	Cr.	Bal.
Balance Forward				106
[2] Dec	PJ		210	
[6] Dec	CD	158		158

Purchases

Mo.	Jr.	Dr.	Cr.	Bal.
Balance Forward				1983
[1] Dec	PJ	183		2166

Purchases Discounts

Mo.	Jr.	Dr.	Cr.	Bal.
Balance Forward				42
[7] Dec	CD		4	46

Prepaid Rent

Mo.	Jr.	Dr.	Cr.	Bal.
Balance Forward				0
[3] Dec	PJ	8		8
[12] Dec	GJ		4	4

Rent Expense

Mo.	Jr.	Dr.	Cr.	Bal.
Balance Forward				44
[11] Dec	GJ	4		48

Delivery Equipment

Mo.	Jr.	Dr.	Cr.	Bal.
Balance Forward				60

Repair Expense

Mo.	Jr.	Dr.	Cr.	Bal.
Balance Forward				56
[4] Dec	PJ	13		69

Utility Expense

Mo.	Jr.	Dr.	Cr.	Bal.
Balance Forward				56
[5] Dec	PJ	6		62

Postage Expense

Mo.	Jr.	Dr.	Cr.	Bal.
Balance Forward				44
[9] Dec	CD	5		49

Travel Expense

Mo.	Jr.	Dr.	Cr.	Bal.
Balance Forward				51
[10] Dec	CD	6		57

Depreciation Expense

Mo.	Jr.	Dr.	Cr.	Bal.
Balance Forward				0
[16] Dec	GJ	15		15

Accumulated Depreciation

Mo.	Jr.	Dr.	Cr.	Bal.
Balance Forward				45
[17] Dec	GJ		15	60

This page is intentionally blank.

CHAPTER 5

Payroll Cycle

This chapter discusses the transactions, documents, and records in the payroll cycle. First, an overview is provided for each of the two subcycles of the overall cycle. The remainder of the chapter concerns the actions in each subcycle and the transactions resulting from those actions.

The payroll cycle could be considered a part of the purchases and cash disbursements cycle. The receipt of employment services is similar to receiving services from outside repairmen or consultants. Payroll is considered a separate cycle because of several unique characteristics:

- Employees are normally retained on a long-term basis.

- Disbursements to employees require a special consideration because of tax withholding laws and fringe benefit considerations.

- Most companies maintain a separate bank account for payroll and a separate journal for payroll disbursements (payroll journal).

- Both the purchase of and cash disbursements for payroll services are usually recorded at the same time and in the same journal, rather than in separate journals. The reason is the short time span between the purchase of employee services and payment for the services.

The payroll cycle starts with the employment of personnel and ends with the periodic payment and recording of the payments for the services rendered.

SUBCYCLES, ACTIONS, COMMON TRANSACTIONS, AND TYPICAL ACCOUNTS AFFECTED

There are only two subcycles in the payroll cycle. Most of the actions take place in the first subcycle. The recording of these actions results in transactions, which in turn result in changes in account balances. The two subcycles are shown below.

Subcycles	Actions	Common Transactions	Typical Account Balances Affected
Receipt and payment of employee services	Hire employees, receive employee services, process time cards, pay employees, record payroll disbursements in journal and subsidiary ledger, summarize and post to general ledger.	Disbursements for employee services	Cash Wages and salaries expense Withholding taxes payable Payroll taxes payable
Payroll accruals	Determine accruals for payroll and payroll taxes, record in general journal and post to general ledger.	Payroll accrual Payroll tax accrual	Wages and salaries expense Wages and salaries payable Payroll tax expense Payroll taxes payable

ACCOUNTANT'S OBJECTIVES

The accountant's objectives in recording transactions in the payroll cycle and summarizing the resultant account balances are almost the same as for purchases and cash disbursements. They are as follows:

1. All existing payroll transactions are recorded.

2. All transactions are recorded and summarized at the correct amounts.

3. All transactions are correctly classified as defined by the chart of accounts.

4. All transactions are included in the proper period.

5. Accrued payroll and payroll taxes at the balance sheet date are stated at the correct amounts.

6. All material disclosures affecting the accounts are included in the financial statements and related footnotes.

RECEIPT OF AND PAYMENT FOR EMPLOYEE SERVICES — ACTIONS AND RELATED DOCUMENTS

Figure 5-1 includes a flowchart of the actions and related documents for receiving and paying for employee services in a typical company. Discussion of the information in the flowchart follows.

FIGURE 5-1
Receipt of and Payment for Employee Services — Actions and Related Documents

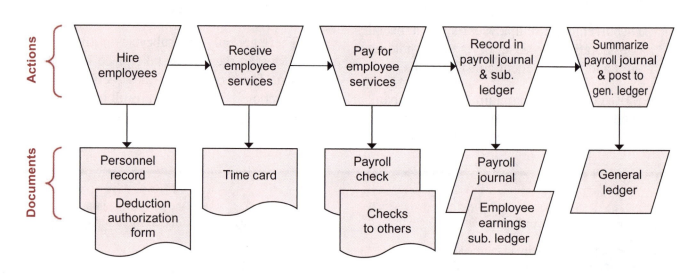

ACTIONS	DOCUMENTS
Hire employees — Employees are interviewed and hired to meet a firm's employment needs. There must be agreement between a company and a new employee of the regular and overtime wage rate, fringe benefits, and the amount of withholding for such items as income taxes, hospitalization, insurance, and union dues.	**Personnel record** — A record including such data as the date of employment, regular and overtime pay, authorized deductions, and termination of employment. *(continued on following page)*

ACTIONS	DOCUMENTS
	Deduction authorization form — A form prepared by an employee authorizing payroll withholding for such items as income taxes, union dues, and retirement savings.
Receive employee services — Some employees work on a monthly basis. Frequently they are paid for overtime. Other employees are paid on an hourly, commission, or piece-rate basis.	**Time card** — A document prepared by an employee indicating the time an employee started and stopped working each day and the number of hours worked. This document is usually generated by a time clock.
Pay for employee services — There are four elements of paying for employee services: 1. Summarize the time cards and calculate the gross pay, withholdings, and net pay for each employee. 2. Prepare and distribute payroll checks. 3. Make disbursements for withholdings from employees. 4. Calculate and pay employer payroll taxes and fringe benefits.	**Payroll check** — A document prepared to pay an employee for employment services performed. The check is for the net pay, after deducting withheld taxes and other items such as medical insurance and union dues. After the check is cashed and returned to the company by the bank, it is referred to as a cancelled payroll check. **Checks to others** — Documents prepared to pay the federal or state government, union, or other organization for payroll-related services. These are of two types: • Withholdings from employees. • Employer payroll taxes and fringe benefit expenses. These checks are usually paid from the general cash account rather than the payroll account.
Record in payroll journal and subsidiary ledger — The payroll journal is the record of original entry for payroll transactions. Every payroll check disbursement must be recorded in the payroll journal, individually or in summary form. Every payroll transaction must also be recorded in the employee earnings subsidiary ledger. The company is responsible for keeping records to enable it to prepare employee W-2 forms annually and to demonstrate it has complied with federal and state employment regulations.	**Payroll journal** — A journal for recording payroll disbursements. It frequently has separate columns to indicate regular pay, overtime pay, each type of withholding, net pay, check number, and the account classification. **Employee earnings subsidiary ledger** — A ledger for recording accumulated payroll information for each employee. The same information shown in the payroll journal is also included in the subsidiary ledger. The difference is that an employee earnings subsidiary ledger (accumulated payroll record) is prepared for each employee for the year. A new earnings record is started for an employee each year.
Summarize payroll journal and post to general ledger — The concepts are the same as for all other journals.	**General ledger** — See Sales (page 37) and Purchases (page 55).

PAYROLL AND PAYROLL TAX ACCRUALS — ACTIONS AND RELATED DOCUMENTS

When periodic financial statements are prepared, it is usually necessary to accrue payroll and payroll taxes. Generally accepted accounting principles require accrual of payroll and payroll taxes in the period employees work, rather than when cash is disbursed. The accrual is normally left on the books until the end of the next accounting period. The actions and related documents for the periodic payroll and payroll tax accruals are shown in Figure 5-2. Discussion of the information in the flowchart follows.

FIGURE 5-2
Payroll and Payroll Tax Accruals — Actions and Related Documents

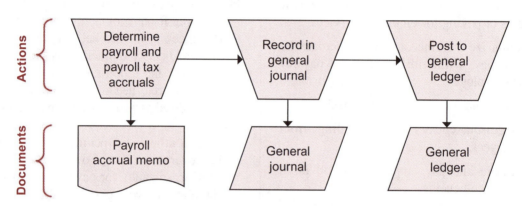

ACTIONS	DOCUMENTS
Determine payroll and payroll tax accruals — Ordinarily there is no payroll expense accrual for employees paid on a monthly basis because they are paid on the last day of the month. An exception is for the unpaid overtime at the end of a period. Hourly employees are often paid weekly or biweekly, usually on a Friday. In that case, an accrual is needed for those hours worked for which payment has not been made at the balance sheet date. Payroll tax and fringe benefit accruals are common. Most companies do not pay the taxes and fringes until the month after the related wages are paid. Proper matching of expenses and revenues requires that these be accrued.	**Payroll accrual memo** — A document prepared indicating the amount of payroll and payroll tax accrual for a period. Many companies do not prepare this document. Instead, the explanation of the calculation can be shown in the general journal. A separate file is usually maintained showing the basis on which the periodic adjustment is made.
Record in general journal — The concepts are the same as those discussed for accruals in Chapter 4.	**General journal** — See Accruals (page 60).
Post to general ledger — The concepts are the same as those discussed in other cycles.	**General ledger** — See Sales (page 37) and Purchases (page 55).

INTERNAL CONTROLS

The following are the most important internal controls for the payroll cycle:

Adequate documents and records. The use of formal time cards for recording regular and overtime hours and the payment of all payroll transactions by check rather than currency are important payroll internal controls. Both of these documents should be prenumbered and carefully controlled. Other special characteristics of adequate documents and records were discussed in Chapter 1.

Authorization of transactions. Authorization by a responsible person is needed at the following points:

- Hiring of personnel. It is necessary that only people with adequate qualifications be authorized to work for the company.

- Wage rate. The rate of pay must be set by an appropriate person in the company.

- Regular and overtime hours. All hours should be approved for each payroll period by a responsible person familiar with the work that is being done.

- Dismissal of personnel. Controls are needed to assure that employees are dismissed when no longer needed. More importantly, they should not be paid after dismissal.

Use of time clocks. An important control to prevent fraudulent or unintentional misstatement of time worked is an automatic time clock for hourly employees. There should also be controls to insure that employees clock-in only their own time cards.

Segregation of duties. The following individuals should not handle or have access to signed payroll checks: personnel who authorize hiring or dismissing staff, anyone who collects or approves time cards, and anyone with responsibility for preparing the payroll checks, related accounting records, or payroll bank reconciliation. The segregation of duties is intended to minimize the likelihood of fraud.

Imprest payroll cash. Many companies control the payroll cash by using an imprest bank account, which is separate from the general cash bank account. In an imprest payroll account, there is only one type of cash receipt and one type of cash disbursement.

> Cash receipt — A weekly transfer on the payroll payment date from the general cash account. After the total gross payroll, withholding for income taxes, and other deductions are calculated, transfer is made from the general cash bank account to the payroll bank account of the net amount of the checks to the employees.

> Cash disbursements (employee checks) — After all employees have cashed their checks, the amount of the balance in the payroll account is zero, unless a constant balance is maintained. Most companies keep a small balance, such as $500, in the imprest account.

> When an imprest payroll account such as the one described above is used, payments to the government and others for withheld income taxes, payroll taxes, and fringe expenses are paid from the general cash account.

Independent checks on performance. There are many opportunities for independent checks in the payroll cycle. Three examples are listed:

1. Prepare an independent bank reconciliation.

2. Recalculate hours shown on time cards, compare wage rates to union contracts, and compare withholdings to income tax withholding tables.

3. Account for all payroll time cards and checks.

SUMMARY

Chapter 5 is a study of:

- The nature of the transactions in the payroll cycle.

- The documents and records used to record and summarize transactions in the cycle.

- A method of recording payroll transactions.

- Common internal controls for the cycle.

To better understand the chapter material, a comprehensive example of the relationships among the different parts of the cycle is provided in Figure 5-3 (page 75). Two simple transactions are used to illustrate the most common documents and records in the cycle, and the way the documents are used to record transactions.

A suggested method of studying the material in Figure 5-3 is to trace each transaction from its source to its final recording in the general ledger. After the documents, records, and recording methods in Figure 5-3 are understood, the totals in each general ledger account should be traced to the year-end worksheet in Figure 1-8 on page 18. Notice that the shaded portion of each general ledger account shows the adjusting entries. The balance above the shaded area will therefore be in the unadjusted trial balance columns and the final ledger balance will be in the adjusted trial balance columns in Figure 1-8.

FIGURE 5-3
Illustrative Payroll Cycle Transactions Using Documents
and Records Commonly Found in the Cycle

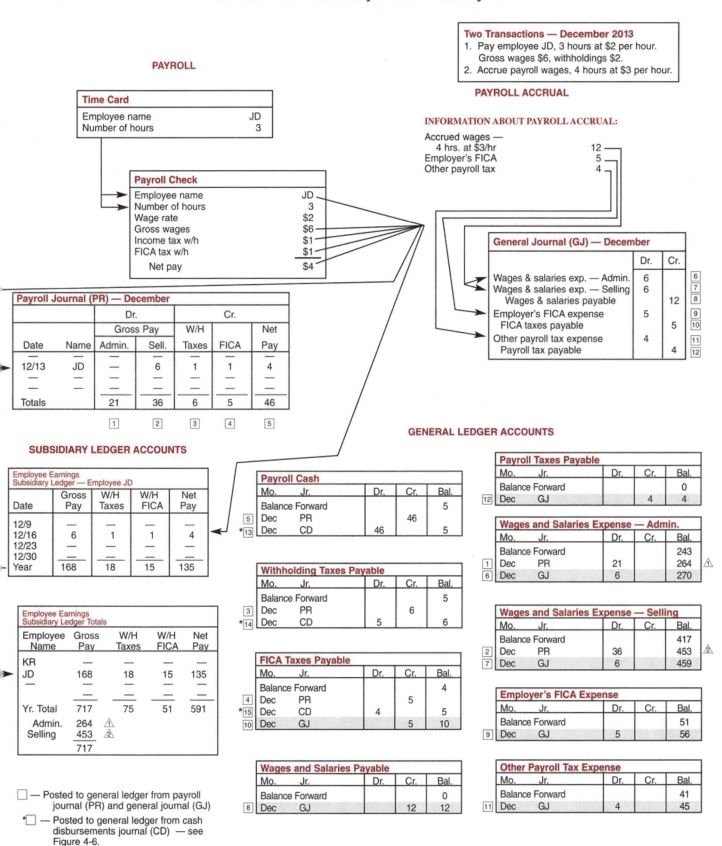

Two Transactions — December 2013
1. Pay employee JD, 3 hours at $2 per hour.
   Gross wages $6, withholdings $2.
2. Accrue payroll wages, 4 hours at $3 per hour.

PAYROLL

Time Card

| Employee name | JD |
| Number of hours | 3 |

PAYROLL ACCRUAL

INFORMATION ABOUT PAYROLL ACCRUAL:

Accrued wages —	
4 hrs. at $3/hr	12
Employer's FICA	5
Other payroll tax	4

Payroll Check

Employee name	JD
Number of hours	3
Wage rate	$2
Gross wages	$6
Income tax w/h	$1
FICA tax w/h	$1
Net pay	$4

General Journal (GJ) — December

	Dr.	Cr.	
Wages & salaries exp. — Admin.	6		6
Wages & salaries exp. — Selling	6		7
Wages & salaries payable		12	8
Employer's FICA expense	5		9
FICA taxes payable		5	10
Other payroll tax expense	4		11
Payroll tax payable		4	12

Payroll Journal (PR) — December

		Dr.		Cr.		
		Gross Pay		W/H		Net
Date	Name	Admin.	Sell.	Taxes	FICA	Pay
12/13	JD	—	6	1	1	4
		—	—	—	—	—
Totals		21	36	6	5	46
		[1]	[2]	[3]	[4]	[5]

SUBSIDIARY LEDGER ACCOUNTS

Employee Earnings Subsidiary Ledger — Employee JD

Date	Gross Pay	W/H Taxes	W/H FICA	Net Pay
12/9	—	—	—	—
12/16	6	1	1	4
12/23	—	—	—	—
12/30	—	—	—	—
Year	168	18	15	135

Employee Earnings Subsidiary Ledger Totals

Employee Name	Gross Pay	W/H Taxes	W/H FICA	Net Pay
KR	—	—	—	—
JD	168	18	15	135
	—	—	—	—
Yr. Total	717	75	51	591
Admin.	264 △			
Selling	453 △			
	717			

Payroll Cash

	Mo.	Jr.	Dr.	Cr.	Bal.
	Balance Forward				5
[5]	Dec	PR		46	
*[13]	Dec	CD	46		5

Withholding Taxes Payable

	Mo.	Jr.	Dr.	Cr.	Bal.
	Balance Forward				5
[3]	Dec	PR		6	
*[14]	Dec	CD	5		6

FICA Taxes Payable

	Mo.	Jr.	Dr.	Cr.	Bal.
	Balance Forward				4
[4]	Dec	PR		5	
*[15]	Dec	CD	4		5
[10]	Dec	GJ		5	10

Wages and Salaries Payable

	Mo.	Jr.	Dr.	Cr.	Bal.
	Balance Forward				0
[8]	Dec	GJ		12	12

GENERAL LEDGER ACCOUNTS

Payroll Taxes Payable

	Mo.	Jr.	Dr.	Cr.	Bal.
	Balance Forward				0
[12]	Dec	GJ		4	4

Wages and Salaries Expense — Admin.

	Mo.	Jr.	Dr.	Cr.	Bal.
	Balance Forward				243
[1]	Dec	PR	21		264 △
[6]	Dec	GJ	6		270

Wages and Salaries Expense — Selling

	Mo.	Jr.	Dr.	Cr.	Bal.
	Balance Forward				417
[2]	Dec	PR	36		453 △
[7]	Dec	GJ	6		459

Employer's FICA Expense

	Mo.	Jr.	Dr.	Cr.	Bal.
	Balance Forward				51
[9]	Dec	GJ	5		56

Other Payroll Tax Expense

	Mo.	Jr.	Dr.	Cr.	Bal.
	Balance Forward				41
[11]	Dec	GJ	4		45

☐ — Posted to general ledger from payroll journal (PR) and general journal (GJ)

*☐ — Posted to general ledger from cash disbursements journal (CD) — see Figure 4-6.

△ — Subsidiary totals reconcile to control account

75

This page is intentionally blank.

CHAPTER 6

Inventory Cycle

The only major asset found in most financial statements that has not yet been discussed is inventory. The reason for not discussing inventory earlier is that the balance in the general ledger is determined differently in most companies than for other assets. Normally, the inventory balance is determined by counting the inventory and recording the balance in the general ledger through an entry in the general journal. This approach is different from the approach taken for the assets shown below, which have been studied in previous chapters.

| Asset Accounts | Typical Journals for Recording Transactions that Result in Ending Balances | |
	Debits	Credits
Cash in bank	Cash receipts journal	Cash disbursements journal
Accounts receivable	Sales journal	Cash receipts journal
Fixed assets	Purchases journal	Cash receipts journal
Marketable securities	Cash disbursements journal	Cash receipts journal

This chapter contains a discussion of periodic and perpetual inventories and the relationship of inventory to the other cycles.

PERIODIC INVENTORY METHOD

Under the periodic inventory method, the only way to obtain an accurate balance for ending inventory is to count the inventory physically, determine the cost of each inventory item, and calculate the total balance. Cost of goods sold using the periodic inventory method is determined by the formula shown below.

The entire emphasis in accounting for ending inventory and cost of goods sold under the periodic method is determining the ending value of inventory. The steps to determine ending inventory are shown in Figure 6-1 (page 78) and discussed in detail below the figure.

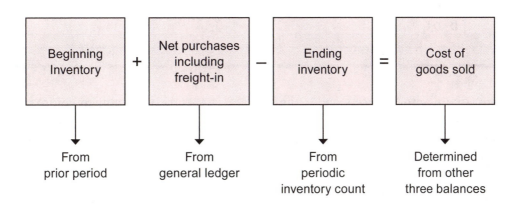

| Beginning Inventory | + | Net purchases including freight-in | − | Ending inventory | = | Cost of goods sold |

From prior period — From general ledger — From periodic inventory count — Determined from other three balances

FIGURE 6-1
Steps in Determining Inventory Using the Periodic Method

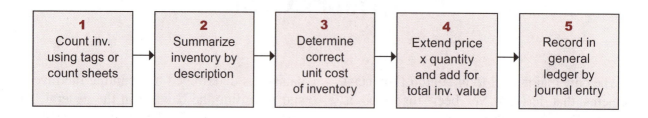

1	2	3	4	5
Count inv. using tags or count sheets	Summarize inventory by description	Determine correct unit cost of inventory	Extend price x quantity and add for total inv. value	Record in general ledger by journal entry

1. **Count inventory.** Company personnel count the inventory on hand at a certain time, ideally on the balance sheet date. You may have encountered an inventory count in progress when you have seen a notice in a store stating: "Closed for Inventory." The quantity and description of inventory on hand can simply be listed on a sheet of paper. A common alternative is to use inventory tags such as the one shown in Figure 6-2. The advantage of using inventory tags is the opportunity for control. First, a person counts the inventory, attaches a tag to the inventory, and records the information on one-half of the tag. Then the person tears off the half with the information on it and keeps it. A second person independently counts the same inventory and records the count on the remaining half of the tag. This time the tag is left on the inventory. After all inventory is counted, a supervisor makes sure that all existing inventory is tagged. All tags are then collected and the two halves are matched, using tag numbers. For any tag where the information on the two halves differs, as it does for the quantity on the tag in Figure 6-2, the inventory is recounted. This procedure provides reasonable control of an accurate inventory count.

FIGURE 6-2
Inventory Count Tag

		Tag 301
Department	Tools	
Description	296	
Quantity	57	
Condition	good	
Counter	D. D.	

		Tag 301
Department	Tools	
Description	296	
Quantity	51	
Condition	OK	
Counter	Phyl	

2. **Summarize inventory.** Frequently, the same type of inventory is found in more than one place, and therefore is counted on separate tags. The cost of inventory by FIFO, LIFO, or weighted-average requires that all inventory of the same type be combined before it is costed. It is also necessary to separate raw materials, work-in-process, and finished goods for financial statement disclosure. It is usually more convenient to do that after the inventory has been counted.

Summarization is easier when tags are used rather than count sheets. Tags can simply be sorted in any way the company wants. Only one inventory description and quantity is put on each tag. It is common to have the information on the tags key-entered for computer processing. Summarization can then be done in any way the company desires.

3. **Determine correct unit cost of inventory.** The proper unit cost depends on the inventory costing method followed and the type of inventory. The unit cost for FIFO will usually be different from that for LIFO or weighted-average. Correct costing must also consider whether freight and handling costs are to be included in inventory. Labor and overhead are also a part of the cost of work-in-process and finished goods inventory.

After the inventory costing method has been determined, the company must determine the correct unit cost of each inventory description. This is done by examining vendors' invoices. For example, assume there are 53 units of purchased part number B1603 on hand at 6-30-13, the year-end date. The following purchases of inventory have occurred:

Date Purchased	Units Purchased	Unit Cost
2-16-13	30	5.80
4-28-13	50	6.05
6-03-13	40	5.95
7-15-13	50	$6.10

The unit cost for the ending inventory using FIFO is 40 units at $5.95 and 13 at $6.05. The 7-15-13 purchase is after the balance sheet date. The cost of $6.10 is therefore not used.

In addition to historical cost, the accountant must be concerned about the lower of cost or market. Some inventory costs may have gone down due to market conditions. Normally, replacement cost is used as the market cost when this occurs. In other situations, the marketability of a product may have declined due to damage or obsolescence. The current selling price of inventory is typically used in that situation.

4. **Extend price times quantity and add totals.** This part of the process is entirely mechanical. Care must be used to make sure that raw material, work-in-process, and finished goods are totaled separately.

5. **Record in general ledger by journal entry.** When the total is determined, it is recorded by an adjusting entry. The entry depends on the way inventory has been recorded in the accounting records. For example, assume ending inventory is $9,000 and the general ledger has the following information at the balance sheet date:

Inventory	$12,000 (from prior period)
Purchases	90,000
Purchases discounts	2,000
Purchases returns	5,000
Freight-in	6,000

The adjusting entry in the general ledger will be:

	Debit	Credit
Purchases discounts	2,000	
Purchases returns	5,000	
Cost of goods sold	92,000	
Purchases		90,000
Freight-in		6,000
Inventory		3,000

The debits to purchases discounts and purchases returns and the credits to freight-in and purchases close those accounts. The debit or credit to inventory adjusts the inventory account to match the ending inventory balance. Cost of goods sold is plugged for the difference (beginning inventory plus net purchases plus freight less ending inventory equals cost of goods sold).

PERPETUAL INVENTORY METHOD

Perpetual inventory records are subsidiary inventory records that tie to the inventory control account. An example of a perpetual inventory record is shown in Figure 6-3 below.

Under the perpetual inventory method, cost of goods sold is calculated for each sale and the residual is ending inventory. The relationship of inventory to purchases and costs of goods sold is different from that shown on page 77. The inventory formula for the perpetual method follows.

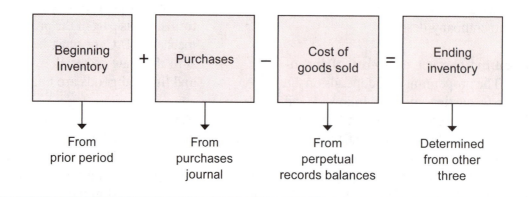

FIGURE 6-3
Perpetual Inventory Record

Product A-11			Inventory Method:		FIFO			
	Receiving or Shipping Number	**Purchased or Returned**			**Sold**		**Balance**	
Date		**Units**	**Unit cost**	**Total**	**Units**	**Dollars**	**Units**	**Dollars**
1-1-13			47.21				36 at 47.21	1,699.56
2-6-13	R62	41	51.67	2,118.47			77	3,818.03
2-9-13	S211				14	660.94	63	3,157.09
3-4-13	R71	28	50.89	1,424.92			91	4,582.01
4-2-13	S340				37	1,813.67	54	2,768.34

Calculating cost of goods sold in Figure 6-3 for the sale on 2-9-13 is simple. Each unit in beginning inventory had a cost of $47.21 and there were more units on hand (36) than units sold (14). Cost of goods sold is therefore $660.94 (14 x $47.21).

The calculation of cost of goods sold is more complex for the 4-2-13 sale, and is shown below.

	Units	Unit Cost	Cost of Goods Sold
On hand, 1-1-13	36	$47.21	
Sold, 2-9-13	14		
Remaining units	22	47.21	$1,038.62
From first purchase (FIFO)	15	51.67	775.05
Total Cost of Goods Sold (4-2-13 Sale)			$1,813.67

When the perpetual inventory method is used, there are two accounting entries for each sales transaction.

1. **Record the sale.** Sales are recorded *at selling price* in the sales journal for the total amount of the sale in the manner described in Chapter 3.

2. **Record the cost of goods sold.** For each sale there is recorded, *at cost*, a debit to cost of goods sold and a credit to inventory. The cost of goods sold entry can be recorded in one of two places.

- Two additional columns in the sales journal, one for the debit to cost of goods sold and the second for the credit to inventory.

- A separate journal with the same two columns as above.

For example, assume the sale on 2-9-13 shown in Figure 6-3 was made by Smith Company to Jones Hardware for $986.26 on credit. Figure 6-4 shows the recording in the sales journal assuming two separate columns for inventory.

FIGURE 6-4
Sales Journal
Including the Columns for Perpetual Inventory

Date	Customer	A/R Dr.	Sales Cr.	COGS Dr.	Inventory Cr.
2-9-13	Jones Hdw.	986.26	986.26	660.94	660.94
		Selling price from Smith to Jones		Purchase price Smith paid original vendor	

BENEFITS OF PERPETUAL METHOD

The reason many companies use the periodic rather than the perpetual inventory method is the higher record keeping costs of the perpetual method. There are, however, certain advantages of the perpetual method:

1. The quantity and dollar value on hand at anytime for any item in inventory can be determined by examining the perpetual records. The lack of inventory records under the periodic method creates problems in maintaining adequate inventory quantities and in determining the ending inventory value.

2. Under the periodic method, the accuracy of the total in cost of goods sold is dependent on the accuracy of recording and determining the beginning and ending balance in inventory. Perpetual inventory records provide a check on the accuracy of the cost of goods sold and a measure of losses through such things as theft and spoilage.

SOURCE OF INFORMATION IN THE PERPETUAL RECORDS

When the documents and records for sales and cash receipts (Chapter 3) and purchases and cash disbursements (Chapter 4) were discussed, perpetual inventory was ignored. That was done for simplicity. Now the documents and records in those cycles are expanded to include the perpetual records. Figure 6-5 (page 82) shows the subcycles in the two cycles that affect perpetual

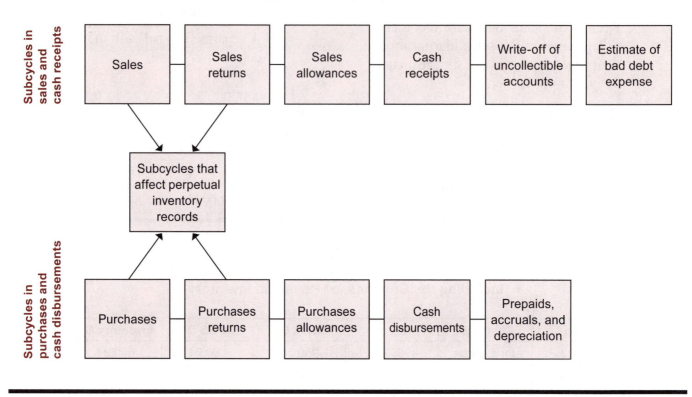

FIGURE 6-5
Relationship of Perpetual Inventory to Sales,
Sales Returns, Purchases, and Purchases Returns

records. There are only four subcycles that affect the perpetuals:

Sales (inventory items only)

Sales returns (not sales allowances)

Purchases (inventory items only)

Purchases returns (inventory returns only)

Figure 6-7 (page 85) shows the relationship between the actions and documents and records for sales (see Figure 3-1) and for purchases (see Figure 4-1) to perpetual inventory (see Figure 6-3). Sales and purchases returns are not shown, but the concepts are the same as for sales and purchases. As shown in Figure 6-7, the sources of information in the perpetual records for purchases of inventory are receiving reports and vendors' invoices. A receiving report states the quantity of goods received, whereas a vendor's invoice includes the unit and total cost. The source of information for reductions in the quantities in the perpetual records, as indicated by Figure 6-7, is the bills of lading, which are prepared as a part of sales. Cost of goods sold on the perpetual records is determined by calculation, depending on the inventory method (FIFO, LIFO, weighted-average).

PHYSICAL COUNT WHEN THERE ARE PERPETUAL RECORDS

The perpetual records reflect the quantity of inventory on hand at any point in time. Periodically most companies take a physical count of the actual inventory for comparison to the perpetuals. The perpetuals are then adjusted to the actual quantity on hand. The primary reasons for differences between the quantities on physical count and perpetual records are record keeping errors and theft of inventory. Naturally, a company should investigate significant differences between the physical count and the perpetual records. The frequency of a physical count depends on the number, frequency and size of past differences between the actual count and the perpetual records.

The total cost of inventory on hand at the balance sheet date is determined from the perpetual records, assuming the company believes the perpetuals are accurate. The quantities can be determined far more quickly from perpetuals than by a physical count.

DETAILED PERPETUAL INVENTORY RECORDS

Many companies keep a record of the units and unit costs of each type of inventory, without keeping a record of the dollar balance. An example is shown in Figure 6-6. These records are called detailed perpetual inventory records, but a company using them is not using the perpetual method of determining inventory. The perpetual inventory method requires that cost of goods sold be calculated for each sale and the subsidiary inventory records equal the inventory control account.

These detailed perpetual records provide a current record of inventory on hand and unit costs without the time and cost of using the perpetual inventory method.

FIGURE 6-6
Perpetual Inventory Records — Units and Unit Costs Only

Product A-11					
Date	Receiving or Shipping Number	Unit Cost	Purchased	Sold	Balance
1-1-13		47.21			36
2-6-13	R62	51.67	41		77
2-9-13	S211			14	63
3-4-13	R71	50.89	28		91
4-2-13	S340			37	54

INTERNAL CONTROLS

Several internal controls related to inventory have already been discussed in previous chapters. Examples include proper authorization of purchases and sales, adequate receiving reports and shipping documents, and internal verification. Other important internal controls for inventory are as follows:

Perpetual records. Well-prepared perpetual records provide a record of inventory to help a company control inventory stock levels. They are also useful in determining whether there is theft of inventory by customers, vendors, or employees.

Segregation of duties. The person who is responsible for inventory should not be responsible for maintaining the perpetual records or other accounting records. For example, the person who receives inventory should not record the purchase in the perpetual records or the accounts payable records. Similarly the person responsible for shipping merchandise to customers should not record the sale in the perpetual records or the accounts receivable records. Any of these incompatible duties provides the person an opportunity to take the inventory for personal gain. Due to the overlap of responsibility, there would be little chance of uncovering the theft.

Safekeeping of inventory. Whenever practical, inventory should be safeguarded to prevent theft or misuse. For inventory such as diamonds, the need for keeping them safeguarded at all times is obvious. It is more difficult, but also important, for inventories of such things as large tires and supplies to be protected. Many companies keep inventory under the supervision of a custodian in a location that can be locked at night.

Independent checks on performance. There are several opportunities for independent checks in other aspects of inventory besides those discussed in previous chapters for purchases and sales. Two examples are as follows:

- Second counts of inventory by an independent count team during the periodic inventory count.

- Recalculation of unit and total costs of inventory on the physical inventory summaries.

SUMMARY

Chapter 6 is a study of:

- The nature of the transactions in the inventory cycle.

- The documents and records used to record and summarize transactions in the cycle.

- A method of recording inventory transactions.

- Common internal controls for the cycle.

To better understand the chapter material, a comprehensive example of the relationships among the different parts of the cycle is provided in Figure 6-8 (pages 86 and 87). Three simple transactions are used to illustrate the most common documents and records in the cycle and how the documents are used to record transactions.

A suggested method of studying the material in Figure 6-8 is to trace each transaction from its source to its final recording in the general ledger. Special emphasis should be placed on examining the source of the information in the physical inventory summary and the periodic inventory adjustment.

After the documents, records, and recording methods in Figure 6-8 are understood, the totals in each general ledger account should be traced to the year-end worksheet in Figure 1-8 on page 18. Notice that the shaded portion of each general ledger account shows the adjusting entries. The balance above the shaded area will therefore be in the unadjusted trial balance columns and the final ledger balance will be in the adjusted trial balance columns in Figure 1-8.

FIGURE 6-7
Perpetual Inventory (Sales and Purchases) — Actions and Related Documents

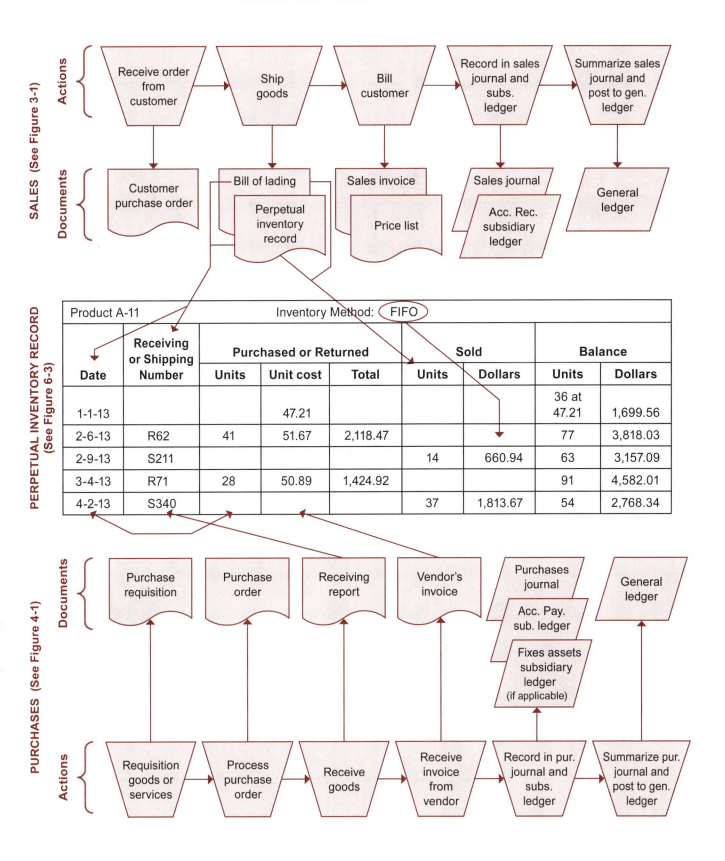

SALES (See Figure 3-1)

Actions

| Receive order from customer | → | Ship goods | → | Bill customer | → | Record in sales journal and subs. ledger | → | Summarize sales journal and post to gen. ledger |

Documents

Customer purchase order

Bill of lading / Perpetual inventory record

Sales invoice / Price list

Sales journal / Acc. Rec. subsidiary ledger

General ledger

PERPETUAL INVENTORY RECORD (See Figure 6-3)

Product A-11   Inventory Method: FIFO

Date	Receiving or Shipping Number	Purchased or Returned — Units	Unit cost	Total	Sold — Units	Dollars	Balance — Units	Dollars
1-1-13			47.21				36 at 47.21	1,699.56
2-6-13	R62	41	51.67	2,118.47			77	3,818.03
2-9-13	S211				14	660.94	63	3,157.09
3-4-13	R71	28	50.89	1,424.92			91	4,582.01
4-2-13	S340				37	1,813.67	54	2,768.34

PURCHASES (See Figure 4-1)

Documents

Purchase requisition

Purchase order

Receiving report

Vendor's invoice

Purchases journal / Acc. Pay. sub. ledger / Fixes assets subsidiary ledger (if applicable)

General ledger

Actions

| Requisition goods or services | → | Process purchase order | → | Receive goods | → | Receive invoice from vendor | → | Record in pur. journal and subs. ledger | → | Summarize pur. journal and post to gen. ledger |

85

FIGURE 6-8
Illustrative Inventory Cycle Transactions
Using Documents and Records Commonly Found in the Cycle

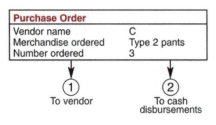

PURCHASES (See Figure 4-6)

Purchase Order

Vendor name	C
Merchandise ordered	Type 2 pants
Number ordered	3

①
To vendor

②
To cash
disbursements

Receiving Report

Vendor name	C
Merchandise received	Type 2 pants
Number received	3

①
To cash
disbursements

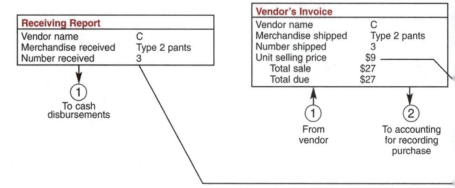

Vendor's Invoice

Vendor name	C
Merchandise shipped	Type 2 pants
Number shipped	3
Unit selling price	$9
Total sale	$27
Total due	$27

①
From
vendor

②
To accounting
for recording
purchase

SALES (See Figure 3-9)

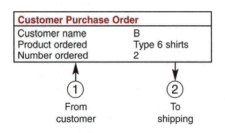

Customer Purchase Order

Customer name	B
Product ordered	Type 6 shirts
Number ordered	2

①
From
customer

②
To
shipping

Bill of Lading

Customer name	B
Product shipped	Type 6 shirts
Number shipped	2

①
To
customer

②
To
billing

③
To
perpetual
records

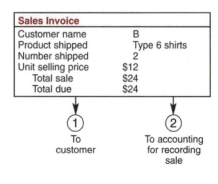

Sales Invoice

Customer name	B
Product shipped	Type 6 shirts
Number shipped	2
Unit selling price	$12
Total sale	$24
Total due	$24

①
To
customer

②
To accounting
for recording
sale

PERIODIC INVENTORY ADJUSTMENT

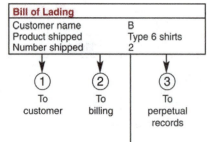

INFORMATION ABOUT PERIODIC INVENTORY ADJUSTMENT:

Balance in inventory per
physical inventory
summary $114

General Journal (GJ)

	Dr.	Cr.	
Inventory		12	1
Cost of goods sold	2132		2
Purchases		2166	3
Purchases discounts	46		4

☐ — posted to general ledger

86

Three Inventory Transactions — December 31

1. Purchase — 3 type 2 pants at $9 each — Vendor C
   (see Figure 4-8)
2. Sale — 2 type 6 shirts at $12 each — Customer B
   (see Figure 3-9)
3. Periodic inventory adjustment for end of year balance per
   perpetual records

PERPETUAL INVENTORY RECORDS

GENERAL LEDGER ACCOUNTS

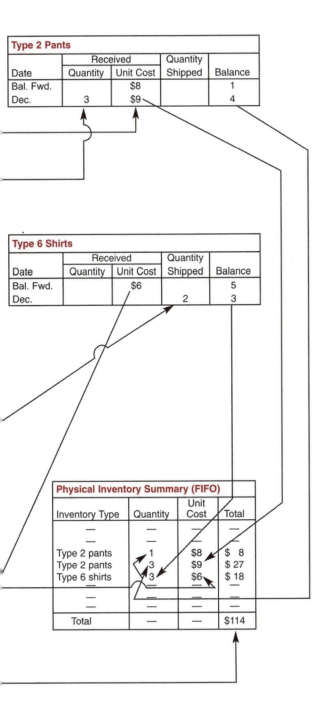

Type 2 Pants

Date	Received Quantity	Received Unit Cost	Quantity Shipped	Balance
Bal. Fwd.		$8		1
Dec.	3	$9		4

Type 6 Shirts

Date	Received Quantity	Received Unit Cost	Quantity Shipped	Balance
Bal. Fwd.		$6		5
Dec.			2	3

Physical Inventory Summary (FIFO)

Inventory Type	Quantity	Unit Cost	Total
—	—	—	
—	—	—	
Type 2 pants	1	$8	$ 8
Type 2 pants	3	$9	$ 27
Type 6 shirts	3	$6	$ 18
—	—	—	—
—	—	—	—
Total	—	—	$114

Inventory

Mo.	Jr.	Dr.	Cr.	Bal.
Balance Forward				126
[1] Dec.	GJ		12	114

Purchases

Mo.	Jr.	Dr.	Cr.	Bal.
Balance Forward				1983
Dec.	PJ	183		2166
[3] Dec.	GJ		2166	0

Purchases Discounts

Mo.	Jr.	Dr.	Cr.	Bal.
Balance Forward				42
Dec.	CD		4	46
[4] Dec.	GJ	46		0

Cost of Goods Sold

Mo.	Jr.	Dr.	Cr.	Bal.
[2] Dec.	GJ	2132		2132

This page is intentionally blank.

CHAPTER 7

Statement of Cash Flows

A statement of cash flows is required for financial statements prepared in accordance with generally accepted accounting principles. The statement shows the increases and decreases in cash and cash equivalents for an accounting period. Cash includes accounts such as general cash, petty cash and savings accounts. Cash equivalents include short-term highly liquid temporary investments such as certificates of deposit and money market accounts. Assume cash and cash equivalents include general cash of $100 and certificates of deposit of $40. Beginning cash for the same accounts had been $90 and $35 respectively. The statement of cash flows will show the increases of cash and decreases of cash that resulted in the net cash increase of $15.

FIGURE 7-1
Types of Proceeds and Uses of Cash

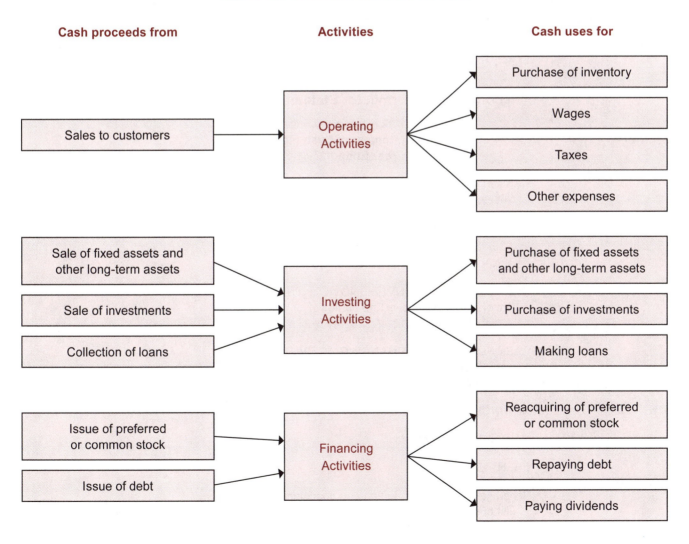

Cash proceeds from   **Activities**   **Cash uses for**

Sales to customers	→	Operating Activities	→	Purchase of inventory
				Wages
				Taxes
				Other expenses

Sale of fixed assets and other long-term assets		Investing Activities	→	Purchase of fixed assets and other long-term assets
Sale of investments	→			Purchase of investments
Collection of loans				Making loans

Issue of preferred or common stock		Financing Activities	→	Reacquiring of preferred or common stock
Issue of debt	→			Repaying debt
				Paying dividends

CLASSIFICATION OF CASH FLOWS

The statement of cash flows classifies cash inflows (proceeds) and cash outflows (uses) into three activities: operating, investing, and financing. The types of proceeds and uses are shown in Figure 7-1 (page 89) and discussed briefly as follows:

- **Operating activities** include the cash effects of most transactions that make up net income. Cash inflows include cash receipts from customers for goods and services. Cash outflows include cash payments for wages, goods and services, and taxes paid.

- **Investing activities** include buying and selling fixed assets, buying and selling marketable securities other than cash equivalents, and making and collecting loans. Cash proceeds include cash received from selling long-term assets and marketable securities and from principal collections on loans. Cash uses include cash paid for purchases of fixed assets and marketable securities and cash loans to borrowers.

- **Financing activities** include obtaining cash from or returning it to owners and obtaining cash from creditors and repaying amounts borrowed. Cash inflows include the proceeds from the issuance of stock and from borrowing. Cash outflows include repayments of loans and payments to owners, including cash dividends.

FORMAT FOR STATEMENT OF CASH FLOWS

The suggested format for a statement of cash flows is shown in Figure 7-2. The three categories of activities in the statement are the same as those in Figure 7-1, in the same order.

FIGURE 7-2
Recommended Format for Statement of Cash Flows

Anycompany, Inc.
Statement of Cash Flows
Year Ended 12-31-13

CASH FLOWS FROM OPERATING ACTIVITIES	
Net income (loss)	$xxxx
Adjustments to reconcile net income (loss) to net cash from operating activities	
(list of individual inflows and outflows)	xx
Net cash provided by (used in) operating activities	xxx
CASH FLOWS FROM INVESTING ACTIVITIES	
(list of individual inflows and outflows)	
Net cash provided by (used in) investing activities	xxx
CASH FLOWS FROM FINANCING ACTIVITIES	
(list of individual inflows and outflows)	
Net cash provided by (used in) financing activities	xxx
NET INCREASE (DECREASE) IN CASH	xx
CASH - Beginning of year	xx
CASH - End of year	$ xx
Schedule of noncash investing and financing transactions	
(list of individual items)	$ xxx

Cash provided from investing and financing activities must be shown separately from the uses of cash in these two categories. For example, if a company borrows $50,000 and repays $35,000 in the same year, $50,000 is a cash inflow from financing activities and the $35,000 is a cash outflow.

NONCASH INVESTING AND FINANCING TRANSACTIONS

Companies often purchase long-term assets or settle liabilities in ways other than by the use of cash. Common examples are buying a building by taking out a mortgage and purchasing equipment through a long-term loan payable. Activities such as these do not result in increases or decreases of cash, but noncash investing and financing transactions must be disclosed in a separate part of the cash flow statement or in the footnotes to the financial statements. These activities are important information to users and are likely to result in future cash receipts or disbursements. Figure 7-2 shows an appropriate way to include noncash investing and financing transactions.

DIRECT VERSUS INDIRECT METHOD

The direct and indirect methods of preparing a statement of cash flows define alternative ways to present cash flows from operating activities. Both methods present cash flows from investing and financing activities in the same way. Figure 7-3 illustrates the format for the operating activities section of a statement of cash flows using both the direct and indirect methods. Notice that both methods result in an identical net cash flow provided by operating activities. Either of the two methods are acceptable for presentation in

FIGURE 7-3
Direct and Indirect Methods of Presenting Net Cash Flows from Operating Activities

Small Company
Cash Flows from Operating Activities
Direct Method
Year Ended December 31, 2013

Cash receipts from sales		$ 85
Cash payments for:		
Purchases	$ 28	
Operating expenses	13	
Income taxes	6	47
Cash flows provided by operating activities		$ 38

Small Company
Cash Flows from Operating Activities
Indirect Method
Year Ended December 31, 2013

Net income		$ 23
Adjustments to reconcile net income (loss)		
to net cash from operating activities:		
Depreciation	$ 16	
Gain on sale of fixed assets	(5)	
(Increase) decrease in assets:		
Accounts receivable	6	
Inventory	(12)	
Increase (decrease) in liabilities:		
Accounts payable	9	
Accrued liabilities	2	
Income taxes payable	(1)	15
Cash flows provided by operating activities		$ 38

accordance with generally accepted accounting principles.

The indirect method is somewhat easier to prepare. It starts with net income and makes adjustments for the differences between the accrual and cash basis methods of accounting. The direct method requires an adjustment to each account in the income statement for differences between the accrual and cash basis. The remainder of the chapter discusses primarily the indirect method.

PREPARATION OF A STATEMENT OF CASH FLOWS

The three required financial statements other than the statement of cash flows (balance sheet, income statement, and statement of retained earnings) are all prepared on the basis of the accrual method of accounting. The statement of cash flows requires a conversion from the accrual to the cash basis. For example, if accrual sales are $200 and accounts receivable have increased $15 for the period, cash received from sales is $185.

Because the statement of cash flows is not on the accrual basis, it cannot be prepared directly from the year-end adjusted trial balance. It is normally prepared after the other three required statements have been completed. Two additional sources of information beyond the year-end trial balance are required to prepare the statement of cash flows:

- The post-closing trial balance at the beginning of the period.

- Both the increases and decreases of all balance sheet accounts other than those related to operating activities. For example, only the net change of a current asset such as accounts receivable is needed because it is related to an operating activity, but both the increases in the fixed asset account for purchases and the decreases from disposals are

needed. The changes in accounts related to investing and financing activities are obtained by examining the affected general ledger accounts.

There are several steps in the preparation of the statement of cash flows. The remainder of the chapter illustrates the preparation of the statement of cash flows for Simple Example Company for the year ended 12-31-13. The ending 12-31-13 trial balance for all balance sheet accounts, the 2013 net loss, and the 12-31-12 post-closing trial balance are included in Figure 7-4 (page 94). Figure 7-5 (page 95) uses the changes calculated in Figure 7-4 to allocate the changes to the three types of activities required in the statement of cash flows (operating, investing, and financing). The information in Figure 7-5 is used to prepare the 2013 statement of cash flows in Figure 7-6 (page 96). A comparative statement of cash flows is included in Figure 1-1 on page 9 but only the 12-31-13 statement can be determined from the information provided in Figures 7-4 and 7-5. The following are the steps used to prepare the statement of cash flows:

Determine the net change for the period in cash and cash equivalents. It is usually simple to calculate this change by subtracting the ending balance from the beginning balance for each cash and cash equivalent account and totaling the changes. There are only two cash accounts in Figure 7-4 for Simple Example Company. Cash decreased $10, which is indicated by the credit in the Change in Cash and Cash Equivalents column.

Determine the net change for the period for all other accounts. This step is mechanical, but care must be used to correctly identify each change as a debit or a credit. For example, an increase of an asset is a debit whereas the increase of a liability is a credit. The total of these changes must equal the net change in cash and cash equivalents. These changes are shown for Simple Example Company in Figure 7-4. The total debits of $78 exceed the total credits by $10, which is the same amount as the net decrease in cash.

Determine cash flows from operating activities.
The starting point for calculating cash flows from operations using the indirect method is net income or loss. Accrual basis net income (loss) for Simple Example Company is included in the operating activities column in Figure 7-5 as a loss of $61, which was taken from the trial balance in Chapter 1. The loss is also shown on the financial statements on page 8.

To calculate cash flows from operating activities, accrual basis net income or loss must be adjusted for three types of items:

1. Income statement accounts that do not affect cash flows. The most common example is depreciation expense. Amortization and depletion are other examples. These must be added to net income because they are accrual basis expenses that are not cash expenditures. For Simple Example Company, depreciation expense from the income statement is $15. The amount of depreciation is found on the year-end worksheet for Simple Example Company in Figure 1-8, page 18. This $15 is reflected in Figure 7-5 as an increase in accumulated depreciation.

2. Income statement revenue and expenses that must be presented on the statement of cash flows as investing or financing activities rather than operating activities. The most common examples are gains and losses on the sale of fixed assets and investments. Simple Example Company had none of these items.

3. Adjustments for changes in all noncash current assets and current liabilities related to operating activities. Three types of current assets (net accounts receivable, inventory, and prepaid expenses) and four types of current liabilities (accounts payable, accrued liabilities, withheld taxes, and income taxes payable) are the primary accounts used to reflect the accrual basis of accounting for operating activities. They are therefore also used to convert net income (loss) from the accrual basis to the cash basis.

To illustrate the adjustments, assume accrual basis sales of $100, beginning accounts receivable of $10, and ending accounts receivable of $15. The Company accrued $5 more revenue than it collected during the period; therefore, cash collections must have been $95. When the indirect method is used to prepare the statement of cash flows, instead of decreasing accrual sales by $5, the adjustment is to reduce net income by the increase in accounts receivable of $5. An increase of any of the three asset accounts or a decrease in any of the four liability accounts will therefore be used to decrease accrual basis net income to arrive at cash flow from operations. A decrease of any of the three asset accounts or an increase in the four liability accounts will be used to increase accrual basis net income.

The adjustment to each of the current asset and liability accounts affecting operations for Simple Example Company are included in Figure 7-5. Notice that with one exception (depreciation) all of the adjustments to the net loss in the operating activities column result from this third type of adjustment.

Figure 7-5 indicates that cash provided by operating activities for Simple Example Company was $2 even though there was a net loss of $61. The main reasons are an increase in accounts payable of $23, depreciation of $15, and a decrease in inventory of $12.

Determine cash flows from investing activities.
Primary investing activities for most companies are the purchase and disposal of fixed assets and the purchase and sale of investments. The best way to determine these changes is by analyzing the affected general ledger accounts. For example, all fixed asset and investment accounts should be analyzed to determine the increases and decreases in each account.

After determining the activity in each account, it is necessary to determine the cash expenditures. For example, if a $1 million fixed asset was purchased for $100,000 cash and a $900,000 mortgage, only the $100,000 would be shown as a cash flow for investing activities.

The other $900,000 would be included as a noncash investing transaction at the bottom of the statement of cash flows or in the financial statement footnotes. Figure 7-5 shows that no cash was provided from or used in investing activities for Simple Example Company. The only balance sheet account on the trial balance that is related to investing activities for Simple Example Company is delivery equipment. There was no change in that account.

Determine cash flows from financing activities.

The primary financing activities for most companies include borrowing and repaying debt, payment of dividends, and issuing and retiring equity instruments such as common stock. The same analysis of accounts related to financing activities is necessary as was discussed for investing activities.

Figure 7-5 shows that the only financing activity for Simple Example Company in 2013 was the payment of $12 on notes payable.

Prepare the statement of cash flows. The statement of cash flows is prepared from the information obtained in the preceding pages. The format should follow the one illustrated in Figure 7-2.

For Simple Example Company, the statement of cash flows is prepared from the information included in Figure 7-5. The statement is shown in Figure 7-6. Figure 1-1 on page 9 shows a comparative statement of cash flows for Simple Example Company using the indirect method. The 2013 amounts are from the information provided in Figure 7-5. It is not possible for you to derive the 2012 amounts because the 2011 balance sheet totals are not provided.

FIGURE 7-4
SIMPLE EXAMPLE COMPANY
Changes in Balance Sheet Accounts December 31, 2013 and 2012

Account	12-31-13 Dr	12-31-13 Cr	12-31-12 Dr	12-31-12 Cr	Change in Cash and Cash Equivalents Dr	Change in Cash and Cash Equivalents Cr	Changes in All Other Accounts Dr	Changes in All Other Accounts Cr
101 Cash in bank	$ 78		$ 88			$10		
102 Payroll cash	5		5					
103 Accounts receivable	272		267				$ 5	
104 Allowance for doubtful accounts		$ 41		$ 41				
105 Inventory	114		126					$12
106 Prepaid rent	4		7					3
201 Delivery equipment	60		60					
202 Accumulated depreciation		60		45				15
301 Accounts payable		158		135				23
302 Wages and salaries payable		12		0				12
303 Payroll taxes payable		4		3				1
305 Withholding taxes payable		6		5				1
306 FICA taxes payable		10		9				1
401 Notes payable		0		12			12	
501 Common stock		200		200				
503 Retained earnings		103		103				
Net loss		(61)					61	
	$533	$533	$553	$553	—	$10	$78	$68

CASH FLOW STATEMENT — DIRECT METHOD

Essentially the same information is used to prepare the statement of cash flows using either the indirect or the direct method. The only difference is how the information is used.

Figure 7-7 (page 96) shows the statement of cash flows for Simple Example Company using the direct method. Notice that the format (net cash flows from operating activities, cash flows from financing activities, and the net change in cash) is similar to Figure 7-6. The only difference is in the details of the cash flows from operating activities.

The starting point for the direct method statement of cash flows is the current period income statement. For Simple Example Company, the income statement is included on page 8.

To convert the income statement to a cash basis, the same adjustments are necessary that are included in Figure 7-5, plus an additional one. Three examples illustrate the adjustments.

1. Cash receipts from sales (net sales of $3,252) - increase in accounts receivable ($5) - bad debt expense ($49) = $3,198. Bad debt expense must be deducted because accrual basis sales include sales before considering uncollectible amounts.

2. Cash payments for purchases = cost of goods sold ($2,132) - decrease in inventory ($12) - increase in accounts payable ($23) = $2,097. This amount can also be determined as follows: purchases ($2,166) - purchases discounts ($46) - increase in accounts payable ($23) = $2,097.

3. Cash payments for payroll = wages and salaries expense ($729) - increase in wages and salaries payable ($12) = $717.

FIGURE 7-5
SIMPLE EXAMPLE COMPANY
Information to Prepare a Statement of Cash Flows
12-31-13

		Changes in all accounts except cash	Cash flows provided by (used in) operating activities	Cash flows provided by (used in) investing activities	Cash flows provided by (used in) financing activities
Account					
101	Cash in bank				
102	Payroll cash				
103	Accounts receivable	$ 5	$ (5)		
104	Allowance for doubtful accounts	—			
105	Inventory	(12)	12		
106	Prepaid rent	(3)	3		
201	Delivery equipment	—			
202	Accumulated depreciation	(15)	15*		
301	Accounts payable	(23)	23		
302	Wages and salaries payable	(12)	12		
303	Payroll taxes payable	(1)	1		
305	Withholding taxes payable	(1)	1		
306	FICA taxes payable	(1)	1		
401	Notes payable	12			(12)
501	Common stock	—			
503	Retained earnings	—			
Net loss		61	(61)		
Total provided by (used in)		$ 10	$ 2	$ —	$ (12)

* Depreciation expense

FIGURE 7-6
Statement of Cash Flows for Simple Example Company — Indirect Method

Simple Example Company
Statement of Cash Flows
Year Ended 12-31-13

CASH FLOWS FROM OPERATING ACTIVITIES

Net loss	$ (61)
Adjustments to reconcile net	
loss to net cash from operating activities:	
Depreciation	15
(Increase) decrease in assets:	
Accounts receivable	(5)
Inventory	12
Prepaid rent	3
Increase in liabilities:	
Accounts payable	23
Wages and salaries payable	12
Payroll taxes withheld and payable	3
Net cash provided by operating activities	2

CASH FLOWS FROM FINANCING ACTIVITIES

Payments on notes payable	(12)
NET DECREASE IN CASH	$ (10)
CASH - Beginning of year	93
CASH - End of year	$ 83

FIGURE 7-7
Statement of Cash Flows for Simple Example Company — Direct Method

Simple Example Company
Statement of Cash Flows
Year Ended 12-31-13

CASH FLOWS FROM OPERATING ACTIVITIES

Cash receipts from sales		$ 3,198
Cash payments for:		
Purchases	$ 2,097	
Payroll expense	717	
Payroll taxes	98	
Rent, repairs and utilities	176	
Postage and travel	106	
Interest expense	2	3,196
Net cash flows provided by operating activities		2

CASH FLOWS FROM FINANCING ACTIVITIES

Payments on notes payable		(12)
NET DECREASE IN CASH		$ (10)